# Character Building

# Building

## DAY BY DAY

180 Quick
Read–Alouds
for Elementary
School and
Home

**by**
**Anne D. Mather & Louise B. Weldon**

*Edited by Eric Braun*

free spirit
PUBLiSHiNG®

Helping kids
help themselves™
since 1983

**Library of Congress Cataloging-in-Publication Data**

Mather, Anne D.
    Character building day by day : 180 quick read-alouds for elementary school and home / by Anne D. Mather and Louise B. Weldon.
        p. cm.
    ISBN-13: 978-1-57542-178-0
    ISBN-10: 1-57542-178-X
1. Character—Juvenile literature. 2. Children—Conduct of life—Juvenile literature. 3. School children—Conduct of life—Juvenile literature. I. Weldon, Louise B. II. Title.
    BJ1631.M37 2006
    170'.44—dc22

                                                                                    2005028622

Portions of this book originally appeared in *The Cat at the Door and Other Stories to Live By* (1991) and *The Cats in the Classroom* (1995), by Anne D. Mather and Louise B. Weldon, Hazelden Information and Education Services.

Cover design by Marieka Heinlen
Interior design by Michele Dettloff

10 9 8 7 6 5 4 3 2
Printed in United States of America

**Free Spirit Publishing Inc.**
217 Fifth Avenue North, Suite 200
Minneapolis, MN 55401-1299
(612) 338-2068
help4kids@freespirit.com
www.freespirit.com

# Dedication

For Brian and in memory of John

# Acknowledgments

We would like to acknowledge our editor, Eric Braun, for diligence and creativity; our acquisitions editor, Douglas Fehlen, for generosity and cooperation; Sam Harris for cheerfulness and helpfulness; and Sulou Rose for loyalty and generosity. Thanks to teachers KaTrina Wentzel, Jeff Krause, and Abigail Vare for reading and commenting on the manuscript.

# Contents

# Introduction

In schools everywhere, it's not uncommon to see a character trait of the week or month—such as honesty, cheerfulness, or courage—displayed on bulletin boards, printed in students' day planners, and even posted on marquis at local businesses as entire communities get into the spirit. Teachers and students examine the meaning of each character trait and discuss ways to live up to the best standards of each trait.

The subject they're studying is character education, and in recent years it has become a part of school curricula worldwide. But character education itself is not new. In families and faith communities, adults have long taught children about character. In fact, wherever adults and children are together, grown-ups are teaching kids about character whether they realize it or not. However, finding time in the classroom for character education curriculum can be a challenge in this era of ever-increasing teacher responsibilities and academic standards. Teachers have a responsibility to offer character education that is substantial, even if time alotted for the preparation and teaching of that subject is brief. And, of course, character education remains as important as ever for families (where time together often is limited) and communities. That's why we wrote *Character Building Day by Day*—to provide quick but substantive character education for classrooms, families, faith communities, and youth groups.

## How to Use This Book

*Character Building Day by Day* is a collection of short fictional stories based on the character traits used most frequently in the character education programs we examined in schools and communities in the United States. We've included 36 traits, one for each week of the school year, with five stories about each trait—one for each day of the week.

The stories show kids in true-to-life situations, faced with decisions or circumstances that reflect, change, or help form their character. The stories are designed to be read aloud by an adult leader or student, then discussed by your class, youth group, or family. The stories and discussions will stimulate young people to think about how their actions reflect their character—and about what character is.

In addition to the stories, each of the character trait sections is introduced by a thumbnail description of the trait. We recommend reading this description at the beginning of the week to provide context for the stories, and perhaps referring back to it throughout the week.

The character traits in this book are arranged in alphabetical order so teachers, leaders, parents, or students can easily look up the traits they need. If your school has a word of the week, you most likely can find that word—or a similar one—in this book. Read those stories during the week. If you are using this book independently of another program, or as the basis for your program, you may choose to present traits that correspond to lessons you have planned each week. For example, for a two-week lesson on civil rights, you might read the stories in Fairness one week and those in Integrity the next. Or you might pair studying of World War II with stories from Peacefulness, and Acceptance and Tolerance. If you are using this book at home or in a youth group, you can match up traits with discussions you've had or events you've done or planned. For any audience, matching traits or stories with events on the calendar or in the news can be very effective.

*Character Building Day by Day* is designed to be flexible. The daily story and discussion can be completed in five minutes if that's your schedule, or it can be expanded with activities and/or tied to other lessons to last 30 minutes or more. You can choose the sections and stories you want to use, and you can create your own activities. Following are some tips on basic discussions and activities.

## Leading Discussions

To get the most out of the stories, encourage lively discussion by your class or group after you've read each day's story. Many kids may be shy at first, and creating discussion may be difficult. But if you lead with provocative questions, you'll find most kids love to talk about stories, what they mean, and how they relate to their own lives.

An effective way to begin discussions is to ask for volunteers to summarize what happened in the story. This will get kids thinking in broad terms about what the story means and what the main conflict is. We've also provided Talk About It questions at the end of each story to help stimulate discussion with your class or group. Finally, if time allows, you might continue the discussion with questions like the following:

- How does the story relate to (caring, leadership, responsibility)?
- What decisions did the character in the story make? Were the choices difficult?
- Would you have done the same thing? Why or why not?
- Has something like this ever happened to you? If so, what did you do? (Be sure to let several children answer this question.)
- What does it mean to show (assertiveness, courage, loyalty)?

To clearly demonstrate the character traits, many of the stories in *Character Building Day by Day* end with the main character making a positive decision or doing what might be called "the right thing." Of course, real life isn't always so clear—or easy—and it's critical you acknowledge and address this in your discussions. Encourage children to consider a variety of possible alternative endings, both positive and negative, that could occur in every story. What other decisions could the main character in the story have made? What would have been the result or consequence of that?

Older kids may be ready for more complicated discussions, particularly of how certain character traits affect each other in certain situations. For example, ask students if they can think of a time when it's not possible to be both fair and kind. Or, ask them what they would do if keeping a friend's secret (being trustworthy) means lying to someone else (being dishonest). Or if cooperating on a project means giving up some personal creativity. The right thing to do isn't always clear. Often there isn't one right answer, and asking students to weigh their values in different situations can lead to important discussion.

Encourage a positive and safe atmosphere for discussion, making it clear that all ideas are valid and important. It's okay to disagree, but everyone deserves to be respected—it's unacceptable for students to interrupt or make fun of others. This is particularly important when kids are sharing personal experiences.

## Other Activities

You also can explore the stories and character traits through other activities. Role-playing, in which two or more children act out a situation or conflict, is fun and engaging for kids. You may have them play roles from the story you read that day or, if it's appropriate, have them perform a different story (perhaps based on a lesson you're working on or something that happened in your classroom, family, or group). Older kids can even sit down together and plan their own skit. Alternatively, you may simply ask kids to perform spontaneously with a directive, such as, "Pretend you are in the situation in this story. How do you react?"

Another effective activity is freewriting. Use a Talk About It question or one of the questions from page 3—or another question you think is appropriate—as a prompt, then have students respond in writing in a journal, in a notebook, or on a computer. Freewriting should be limited to one to three minutes, and students should keep writing the entire time. If you're having trouble getting your group to discuss the stories, have them do a brief freewriting activity first. This gets them thinking critically about the story and the character trait and usually opens the door to more engaging discussion.

Other activities to consider include drawing, making posters or other art projects, and brainstorming exercises such as webbing and listing.

Finally, don't be afraid to make adjustments if certain activities work better than others. You're in the best position to judge how well your character program is going, and flexibility is the key to success.

We'd love to hear how this book worked for you. Let us know which stories were popular with your class, group, or family and which ones provoked the most discussion. You can contact us by regular mail or email at:

Free Spirit Publishing
217 Fifth Avenue North, Suite 200
Minneapolis, MN 55401-1299
help4kids@freespirit.com

We hope to hear from you, and we wish you great success in your character education program.

*Anne D. Mather and Louise B. Weldon*

# The Stories

# Acceptance and Tolerance

Acceptance and tolerance mean appreciating and respecting differences in people. When you are accepting and tolerant you understand that others may have different feelings, behaviors, or beliefs from you. You don't judge others because they are different from you. Being accepting and tolerant doesn't mean you have to agree with everyone. It means you respect them, even if they are different from you.

# Corn Flakes and Apple Juice

Matt and Kyle stayed awake until after midnight Friday night. The two friends never seemed to run out of things to do. So Saturday morning they were glad to get to sleep in late. At 10:45 a.m., they got up and sleepily picked their favorite kind of cereal to eat for breakfast. Kyle's mouth was wide with a yawn and his eyes grew almost as wide as he watched Matt pour apple juice over his corn flakes.

"Matt, stop. Wake up! That's the apple juice," he exclaimed.

"I know," Matt said calmly. "I put juice on my cereal because I'm allergic to milk."

"Isn't juice on your cereal gross?" Kyle asked.

"No, it's not gross."

"What would happen if you drank some milk?" asked Kyle.

"I get a really bad stomachache and my sinuses hurt. And milk's in a lot of things, like cheese and chocolate, so I have to be careful."

Kyle let that sink in. Then something dawned on him about Matt's allergy. "If you're allergic to milk, you can't eat ice cream!" he said in horror.

"I have a substitute for that, too," Matt replied, smiling. "It's called sorbet. That was the frozen peach dessert we had last night."

"That was really good," Kyle said. After a few minutes he added, "I'm sorry you have to go through all that. It sounds like a real hassle not to be able to have milk."

## Talk About It

What did Kyle do when he learned of his friend's allergy to milk? How do you think Matt felt about answering Kyle's questions? How did each boy show acceptance toward the other?

# The Cat's Meow

Felicia's cat was very unusual. He suffered a high fever when he was 6 months old, and Felicia and her parents were afraid he might die. They stayed up with him all night, rocking him gently. The cat lived, but his meow changed completely. Now he gave a funny little trill, almost like the sound a spring frog makes. The fever also affected his purr. Now you could hear it only if you put your head right up to his throat.

One afternoon Felicia and her friend Melissa were playing with the cat in the grass. When Melissa heard the cat's unique meow and purr, she said, "Hey, this cat has some special features."

"That's a nice way of putting it," Felicia said. "It sounds better than 'weird,' which is what some people call him."

"I know all about special features," Melissa said. "When I was younger I had one of my own." Melissa told Felicia how her left eyelid used to droop, and how she had trouble focusing her eye straight ahead. She had to wear a patch over her good eye to help strengthen the weak one. Lots of kids teased her and called her a pirate.

"That must've been hard," Felicia said.

"It was at first, but then I started to think of it as my special feature. That made it easier."

## Talk About It

What's the difference between saying someone is "weird" and saying the person has "special features"? Does the difference matter? Why or why not?

# Set of Wheels

**B**arry showed up late for hockey practice and he was mad. It was his sister's fault—she had to be dropped off at physical therapy. Barry's little sister Amanda had muscular dystrophy. He really liked her—most of the time. She was spunky and never felt sorry for herself because she needed a wheelchair. In fact, she called it her "set of wheels" and learned to do tricks like wheelies. Barry thought that was pretty cool.

But other times, like today, he got angry when his sister's needs seemed so much more important than his. Barry was ready on time, but their dad had to take Amanda first. Barry had been late many times because of her—he'd even missed games.

He skated at top speed around the rink, warming up. He tried to concentrate on his stick handling and his skating, but he was still thinking about Amanda. Suddenly he felt a jolt to his body as he crashed into another player and fell hard. He hadn't been paying attention to where he was going. A pain burned up from his right elbow to his shoulder. He'd broken his right arm, the arm he did everything with.

For a while he needed help dressing, bathing, and writing. Barry learned how difficult it was not to be able to reach for things easily and to have to depend on someone else to help with his personal needs. It got him thinking about what life might be like for Amanda in her wheelchair.

continued

# Set of Wheels (continued)

One day in the library, Barry found a book about having a handi-capped brother or sister. He checked it out and read it. In the book he learned some ways to deal with being Amanda's brother and he also gained an even greater respect for his sister.

Barry became very interested in making things easier for Amanda. He decided that when his arm healed he would make her a shelf in her room at a level where she could reach things better. And he would help her find other ways to become more independent.

## Talk About It

Why did Barry gain greater respect for his sister? Have you ever gained respect for someone different from you after learning more about him or her? What happened?

# Really Scary

**B**randon and his friend Nina were walking past a convenience store when someone in the parking lot yelled at them. "Go back to your own country!" a man hollered from his car. Nina put her head down and walked faster. A little confused, Brandon quickly followed.

"What was that man talking about?" Brandon asked when he caught up to Nina.

"Sometimes people say mean stuff to me because of my race," Nina said. "It happens a lot."

"But this *is* your country. Why would he say to go somewhere else?"

"I've heard worse than that. One time someone spray painted mean words on our house. We were afraid someone might try to hurt us."

"That's really scary," Brandon said. He was scared right now. The two walked quickly to Nina's block and down to her home. "Don't you get scared?" Brandon asked.

"A little. But this wasn't bad," Nina said. "Just some guy yelling."

Brandon hugged Nina. "I'm so sorry your family is being treated this way," he said.

## Talk About It

Have you or has someone you know ever experienced anything like Nina did? Why are people intolerant sometimes? What are some ways to help change this?

# Resource Class

It was only the second week of school and resource class was already a big problem for Janey. She hurried into the room to avoid being seen, then sat down and caught her breath. Being in resource class meant only one thing to Janey—that she was different. Twice a day, she was separated from her friends to get extra help with her subjects. And sometimes she was teased by other students as she entered the resource classroom.

"I wish I could make myself invisible when I come through that door," Janey said. "I'm sick of being teased."

The other resource class students nodded. They knew. Ms. Miller, their new teacher, listened. She also knew.

"It's tough feeling different," she said to the class. "I really do understand. I was in resource class when I was in elementary school." Then Ms. Miller told the class they could help each other come up with ways to respond when they were teased.

At first the group thought this was silly and didn't want to do it. But finally Janey volunteered. Janey knew she was smart, but she had problems with reading and writing. When she looked at words on a page, the letters got all jumbled up and backwards in her mind. Her teacher was really nice and let her do assignments by reading answers into a tape recorder and turning in the tape. But other kids teased her and called her a dummy.

Janey's classmates suggested she respond to the teasing by saying this: "I'm not dumb. I understand everything fine. I just have a hard time reading and writing words."

"Nice idea," Ms. Miller said. "That way you *explain* how you're different. And remember, if you don't act upset when you're teased, that also will help. Teasers want you to cry or get really mad—if you don't, they'll get bored with teasing you."

Each student who wanted to get help from classmates had a turn. They found ways to respond to teasing that could help the teasers learn more information about their learning differences.

*This was the best resource class ever*, Janey thought.

## Talk About It

Why do you think some kids make fun of others who they think are different? What can you do to prevent that kind of teasing?

# Assertiveness

Being assertive means sticking up for yourself, and asking for what you need or deserve in ways that are respectful. When you are assertive, you are confident *and* courteous. You stand up for your rights without stepping on the rights of others.

# An Oxygen Mask

Tom dipped a large corn chip into the warm salsa con queso and chowed down. "I'm glad you ordered this," his Uncle Jacob remarked.

Just then Tom smelled cigarette smoke. "Oh gross!" he hollered, making a disgusted face. "What are those people doing smoking at the next table? This is the nonsmoking section!" He covered his face with his arm and glared at the smokers. "I need an oxygen mask so I can breathe." Then he made loud choking noises and pretended to pass out in his chair.

Uncle Jacob sat calmly. "Do you think complaining and acting rude is going to change it?" he said.

"I don't know," Tom shrugged.

His uncle called the server to the table and asked him to tell the smokers they were not in the smoking section. When the server approached the couple, it was obvious they were embarrassed. They had not realized they were in the wrong section.

"Thanks, Uncle Jacob," Tom said as the air cleared.

## Talk About It

What's the difference between how Tom handled the smoking and what his uncle did? Why did Uncle Jacob's way work?

# Best Friends Forever

"Wait up!" LaToya called out to her friend. She wanted to walk with Betsy to gym class, but Betsy walked faster, giggling with Jenny and Gina Miller. During the volleyball game, Betsy picked the Miller twins to be on her team before she picked LaToya.

At lunch LaToya got her tray and found Betsy and the two girls. When she tried to squeeze in at their table, nobody would budge. The other girls were deep in conversation and acted like LaToya wasn't there.

LaToya was glad when the school day was over. Since Jenny and Gina came to their school, Betsy wanted to be around them all the time. She hardly had time for LaToya anymore.

That evening Betsy called LaToya like she always did. She talked about her day and how much fun Jenny and Gina were. LaToya felt a lump in her throat and choked back tears. It would be hard to tell Betsy how she felt, but she didn't want to ignore her feelings. Finally, she decided to speak up. "It hurt my feelings when you ignored me today," she said.

Betsy was surprised. "What do you mean?"

LaToya told Betsy that she felt left out since the Miller twins came to their school. She named some examples, like when they didn't talk to her at the lunch table. "We've been best friends forever and I don't like being treated like this," she added.

There was a long silence and then Betsy apologized. "I didn't know I was doing that," she said. "Can we all hang out together tomorrow?"

## Talk About It

Why is it sometimes hard to tell someone, even your close friend, when he or she has hurt your feelings? Talk about a time something like this happened to you.

# Bus Fuss

Jana plopped down next to the window on the school bus. She was taking a string cheese snack from her backpack when Claire crowded into the seat.

"Move over," Claire said as she wedged between Jana and the window. "I want the window seat."

Jana slowly moved to the aisle. Then she pulled out her mystery book and pretended to read, though she was really thinking. Claire was a good friend, but lately she was pushing Jana around a lot. Claire was bigger and she usually took what she wanted.

Jana began to imagine what she could do tomorrow when Claire wanted her seat. First, Jana imagined herself in a superhero outfit protecting her seat by pushing Claire away. But Jana didn't want to be mean. Then she thought she could just laugh, read her book, and ignore Claire. But she knew that wouldn't work. Jana imagined lots of ways she might claim her seat. By bedtime, she thought she had a good plan.

The next day Claire went for Jana's window seat again. This time Jana sat up straight and looked her in the eye. "Claire," she said, "I like being your friend. You can sit by me if you want. But I'm sitting by the window today."

## Talk About It

What do you think of Jana's solution? What would you have done? Why?

# Soda Bottle Cyclone

Jamal's teacher stood in front of the class and explained how the powerful, twisting winds of a cyclone got started, and the damage one could do. Then Mr. Zorn began giving instructions on how the students could make their own cyclone inside a soda bottle. He made a list of what everyone would need—a two-liter soda bottle, some duct tape, water, food coloring, and a drill.

*Dad will like to help me with this one,* Jamal thought. Then his attention began to drift away. This was his weekend to spend with his dad, and he was excited. There was a great playground next to the building his dad lived in. He got to be outside a lot there, and that was fun. Plus, his dad always cooked out on the grill. Jamal could almost taste that cheeseburger.

He jerked back to attention when he heard Mr. Zorn say, "Okay, class, gather your notebooks and let's head to the library. When you get there, look up the Internet site and print out the directions on how to make a cyclone in a bottle. And no talking from this point on!"

Jamal felt a knot in his stomach as he stood up. He had no idea what the Web site was. He didn't want to ask his teacher to repeat it because then Mr. Zorn would know he hadn't been paying attention. He also knew that if he asked a friend he would get in trouble for talking. But what else could he do? If he didn't get the Web site, he couldn't do the assignment. As the class filed out of the room, Jamal tried to make up his mind about what to do.

## Talk About It

What do you think Jamal should do? Why?

# The Bike Borrower

"Phil always asks to borrow my bike," Carlos told his dad one day while they were cleaning out the garage. "It drives me crazy. He has his own bike, but he just likes my 10-speed better. I want to say no, but I don't want to make him mad. He's my friend."

"Saying no nicely is really hard for most people. There are even books to teach adults how to do it!" his dad said as he hung up the broom and brushed his hands together. "Let's figure out what you can say."

"Well, I want him to know we're still friends," Carlos said, "even if I don't let him ride my bike."

"Okay, that's a good place to start. Tell him that first."

"Then, I guess I should tell him *why* I don't like him riding it."

"Good," said his dad. "That will help him understand. After that, tell him what you want him to do."

"Stop asking to borrow my bike."

"Right."

The next day at the park, Carlos got a chance to try out his plan.

"I know you like my bike," he said to Phil. "And you're a good friend. But I want to ride it. I like it, too. So please don't ask to borrow it anymore."

"Well, if you can't share, then fine!" said Phil, and he sped away around the bend in the path.

When Carlos rode around the curve, Phil was waiting for him. "I'll race you to the pond," Phil said.

## Talk About It

Is it hard to say no to good friends? Why or why not? How does it feel when your friends say no to you?

# Balance

Being balanced means having several different parts of your life that are important to you, without giving any of them too much attention. If you have balance you don't put all of your time into just one or two things, such as sports, TV, surfing the Web—or even homework. You have many parts of your life to handle. When you concentrate too much on just one or two, you don't pay enough attention to other important parts.

# Soccer-Crazy

Tad was crazy about soccer. He lived it, dreamed about it, and most of all he played it—every chance he could. He had a game or a practice almost every day, and he played during recess at school, too. He even read books about soccer.

Saturday, walking home after practice, he passed by his good friend Ronnie's apartment. Bouncing his soccer ball on the pavement, Tad looked up at Ronnie's window. A light was on inside. Tad realized it had been a couple weeks since he and Ronnie had played together, maybe even longer. They used to listen to music and play board games all the time. Ronnie had sent Tad a couple emails recently, but Tad hadn't responded. In fact, Tad hadn't even talked on the phone with Ronnie in ages.

Tad bounced the ball again and it hit a crack in the sidewalk and rolled into the street. Tad suddenly felt very lonely for his friend and the fun they had when they used to hang out all the time.

*I'm going to call him right after dinner,* he thought to himself, *and invite Ronnie over to play tomorrow.* Then he picked up his ball and ran home.

## Talk About It

How can Tad add more balance to his life? What could he do to reconnect with his friend?

# Maxed Out

Keisha's grandma encouraged her and her little sister Denise to keep busy. "I always wanted to play the piano," she said. "But we couldn't afford anything like that. You two have a chance I never had."

Keisha and Denise took a piano lesson each week, plus gymnastics and swimming lessons. And they had to practice piano every day. They also belonged to a 4-H Club.

One week the girls' piano teacher was on vacation, and Keisha used her free afternoon to play with the dog, read a book, and just relax. "Grams," she said that night, "it's so nice to have some time for myself. Today felt like a vacation. Do you think we could cut back on the activities a little?"

"Hmm," said Grandma. "Would you like that, Denise?"

"Yeah!" said Denise. "More free time sounds really good."

"I didn't want to hurt your feelings," Keisha said, "but I don't really like piano. But I know how much you wished you could have played when you were a kid."

"Okay," Grandma said. "Let's look at your schedules and pick your favorite activities—the ones you want to stick with."

## Talk About It

Is down time—time when you don't have to do anything—as important to you as time filled with activities? What happens when you don't have enough down time?

# A Basket of Kittens

Sheila's family just finished a very busy week. The family slept later than usual on Saturday morning, and Dad fixed waffles with strawberries and whipped cream for a special treat. Still, the whole family looked tired as they ate.

Mom had worked late every night that week. Sheila had tried out for sixth-grade band, so she had practiced her clarinet extra hours to prepare. Her brother Desmond had played tennis after high school every afternoon until dark, getting ready for a big tournament.

Sheila knew just what to do to relax. She cleared the breakfast dishes from the kitchen table and took out a puzzle of three kittens in a basket that Desmond had given her for her birthday. That was three months ago and she hadn't had time to start the puzzle yet.

She dumped all the puzzle pieces on the table and started turning them right-side up. Dad pulled up a chair and started matching colors to the photograph on the box. In a few minutes, Desmond joined them. He began finding all the pieces with a straight edge to frame the picture. When Mom came in a little while later, she took the fourth chair at the table and gathered pieces that looked like the shiny black cat on the box top.

"Nothing like a puzzle to help us relax and bring a little balance to a hectic week," Mom said.

## Talk About It

What do you do to relax during busy times? Why is relaxation important?

# Fried Brains

Denzel stretched and leaned back in his chair. He rubbed his eyes. He had been at the computer doing research since he got home from school. He had the highest grades in the fifth grade and he hoped to get the principal's award this year.

He was startled when his older brother Clarence walked in holding a football. "Let's play catch before supper," Clarence said. "It's finally warm enough to be outside."

"I can't," Denzel said. "I've got to study."

"Come on. We'll run some pass plays. I'll be quarterback."

"I need to finish this report," Denzel said, though the idea of playing sounded good.

"All you do is study. Your brain is probably fried," Clarence chided. "I saw a thing on TV that said your brain works better if you get outside and look at three-dimensional things instead of flat surfaces all the time."

Now *that* got Denzel's attention. He imagined his brain working even better with some exercise as he put on his jacket to go outside with his brother.

## Talk About It

How do you balance work and play during the week? Describe a time when doing something physical helped you concentrate on studying or another nonphysical activity.

# On a Tight Rope

As the tightrope walker took his first step onto the wire, the only sound in the circus tent was an exciting drumroll. This part of the circus was Li Ming's favorite. "I just don't understand how a person can balance on a wire for that distance," she whispered to her mom.

"These people start practicing early in their childhood and they practice for hours every day," her mom said.

"That doesn't sound very fun," Li Ming said, her eyes on the acrobat above them.

"I agree," her mom replied. "In order to have balance on the tightrope, they have less balance in the rest of their lives. Remember when you got so stressed studying for your social studies test that you got sick? You studied in all your free time for four days. You needed to do something else—to *balance* out the studying."

"But how can a kid have balance when she has to be in school and do homework most of the time—that's what I'd like to know," Li Ming complained.

"That's a hard question," her mom said. "I think the important thing is to make sure you get enough time for playing and relaxing. That's how a kid keeps balanced."

The tightrope walker reached the other platform and bowed, and Li Ming and the rest of the audience erupted in cheers.

## Talk About It

How do you feel when you're stressed, or off-balance? Describe a time you felt this way. How did you deal with it?

# Being a Good Sport

Being a good sport means knowing and following the rules and playing fair. When you are a good sport you play hard and try to win—but you know winning isn't everything. You are kind to your opponents whether you win or lose. Being a good sport is a way of showing respect for others and the game.

# Concentration

"**Y**ou are absolutely fantastic at this game," said Casey's mom. "You always win." Casey loved playing cards with her mom after school. This was her favorite game: Concentration. It consisted of matching up two cards of the same number. The trick was that the whole deck of cards was spread out on the table upside down. Each turn, you could flip up two cards. If they matched—a pair of 2s, a pair of kings—you kept those cards and took another turn.

"I've heard that young people can really focus on things, but adults have too much on their minds," said her mom. "Maybe that explains it."

Just then, her mom dropped a card. Leaning down to pick it up, she noticed something. Their kitchen table was glass. At a certain angle, you could see the reflection of the cards in the glasstop. After she sat up, she noticed that Casey's vision was right at the table top level. Suddenly she understood why her daughter was such a whiz at Concentration.

"Casey, are you reading the reflections of the cards on the table top?" she asked. Casey hung her head but didn't say anything. "Honey, cheating isn't winning. For a while it may seem like it—but I never had a chance."

"I know," Casey said. "I just really like to hear all the nice things you say about me when I do well."

"But if you cheated, you *didn't* really do well," her mom answered. "So all those nice things I said aren't worth much. Wouldn't you rather get compliments for things you *really* do?"

## Talk About It

Why did Casey cheat at the game? What did her mom mean when she said Casey didn't *really* do well? Have you ever cheated and wished you hadn't? Explain.

# In the Dugout

"Safe!" cried the umpire as he signaled the scorekeeper. "Game over. Yankees 6, Blue Jays 5!"

The two baseball teams lined up on the field and filed past each other. Each kid gave each opponent a high-five and said, "Good game!" Then the Blue Jays team slowly moved to the dugout to gather their bats, helmets, and gloves.

"We stink," said Clay, the first baseman.

"Hey, we played a great game," Marco said.

"But we lost," said Craig.

"We have nothing to be ashamed of," Marco said. "Deandre had that home run. Clay, you played great at first base all night, especially that awesome scoop catch in the third inning. And Craig, you caught that high fly ball over near the bleachers. Lots of kids would have lost that in the lights."

"We did our best," said Eric, the shortstop.

"That's right," added Coach. "And you guys never stopped hustling or trying your hardest. Hold your heads up when you leave this dugout and show you are good sports."

"Okay," Clay said. "I'm just bummed we lost. But we *did* play a good game."

"Practice tomorrow at 6:00," the coach said. "Let's look ahead to winning the next one."

## Talk About It

Why is it sometimes hard to be proud when you lose—even if you do your best?

# The Speech Contest

"I can't believe you beat me," Louie said to Kendall as they ate lunch in the cafeteria. "You must have worked really hard on your speech."

"Nah," Kendall replied, opening his carton of milk. "I jotted down some notes last night, that's about it. Then I got up there and just started talking."

"What?" said Louie. "I worked *so* hard on my speech. I researched my topic, wrote the speech, transferred it to note cards, and practiced it for days. I even made my family sit and listen to me so I could get used to talking in front of an audience."

"Well, talking is one thing that comes naturally to me," Kendall said, laughing. "I get in trouble in class almost every day for talking too much." Kendall thought making a joke about his talking would lighten up the situation. But Louie didn't crack a smile.

"Your speech was great," Kendall went on. "And don't forget you whipped me in the spelling bee last week. You always do."

Louie took a bite of his bologna sandwich and thought about that. "That's true," he said after he swallowed. "And you *are* the best talker I know."

## Talk About It

Why was it hard for Louie to accept that Kendall won the speech contest? Think of a time when you felt like Louie. What happened? Like Kendall with speaking and Louie with spelling, what is a skill that comes easily to you?

# The Loss

"That referee must be blind," Cindy said to Allison and Shannon as they walked off the field.

"Or else he's related to the girls on the other team," Allison added, smirking.

Shannon kicked a rock as she walked off the field. "I wish I had kicked that well during the game," she said.

"Don't be down on yourself," Cindy told her. "The game was unfair anyway."

"Their team wasn't even that good," said Allison. "The only reason they won was because of the lousy ref."

"I don't know," Shannon said. "Their goalie was super. And that wing, the tall one? She was *so* fast."

"She was okay," said Cindy. "They got lucky today."

Shannon was silent for the rest of the walk to the bus. There was more bothering her than losing the game. As the three girls plopped down on the long seat in the back of the bus, she spoke up again. "You guys, we were not our best today. I know there were a couple bad calls, but they beat us by *four goals*. Even if every call was perfect, they would have won. They were really, really good and I don't think we should criticize them. Or the ref."

Her friends didn't say anything, but Shannon felt better for saying what she felt.

## Talk About It

What's the difference between the way Shannon thought about the game and the way her friends did? Why is it sometimes hard to admit to not having done your best?

# The Good Winner

Juan swung around the horizontal bar and stopped at the top of his arc, standing straight up and down on his hands above the bar. He then turned his body, switching the grip of his hands, and swung down and around the opposite direction. He seemed to move his body through the air with ease, letting go of the bar and gracefully regrabbing it in a new grip. To finish his routine, he swung quickly and powerfully around the bar and released himself into the air, somersaulting as he flew, before landing perfectly on his feet. The crowd of parents and other kids gasped and burst into applause. His team was on its way to another first-place finish.

Juan was great at gymnastics. He had a shelf full of trophies and a bulletin board crowded with ribbons. By getting the highest score at most events, he had led his team to many first-place finishes. Everyone knew he was the most talented gymnast on the team. But no one had ever heard Juan brag about himself. He never took credit for the team wins because he knew it took a whole team to win.

Juan walked off the mat toward his waiting teammates and high-fived a couple of them. "Nice job, guys," he said, wiping his sweaty face and hands with a towel. "All our practice is paying off!"

## Talk About It

What does it mean to be a "good winner"? Why do you think people sometimes are not good winners?

# Caring

When you are caring you feel interest or concern for others. Other people's feelings matter to you. You can show you care with your actions—by being kind, generous, forgiving, helpful, and understanding. You can also use words to let people know you care about them.

# The Bully

Morgan stared at the TV and aimlessly changed the channels. Then he flipped through a magazine, but he kept thinking about what he'd seen that day at school. A boy from his sixth-grade class had bullied Brian, a third-grader, on the playground. He called Brian names, pushed him down, and threatened to beat him up if he told anyone. And he said he was going to do it again tomorrow.

Others had seen the bullying, too, but they were scared and didn't want to get involved. They didn't want to be the bully's next victim. Morgan was afraid, too, but he felt terrible. Brian didn't deserve to be treated that way.

Something else was bothering Morgan. He couldn't stand bullies, but he also couldn't stand tattle-tales. If he told, wouldn't he be one?

Finally, Morgan went to visit his neighbor, Jed, an older man he enjoyed talking to. Morgan told Jed about the bully. "But I don't want to be a tattle-tale," he finished.

"I'm glad you told me about this," Jed replied. "Bullies have to be stopped or they just get worse. When you tattle on someone, you're trying to get *him* in trouble. But when you report a bully, you're trying to get someone *out* of trouble. That's a big difference."

## Talk About It

How can reporting a bully be an example of caring? Have you ever seen someone being bullied? What did you do?

# Hang in There

Amy's seventh-grade cousin, Nethra, was really angry. Last year she moved from India to Amy's town in the United States. She had a hard time leaving her old friends and making new ones, but she did it. Then last week Nethra's family moved again. Her dad's job transferred him to a different city, and Nethra had to say good-bye to another set of friends and start all over again. "This is lousy!" Nethra complained to her cousin the day she left. "I don't want to leave my friends again."

She had to say good-bye to Amy, too. The cousins had become close over the last year, and Amy would really miss her. Most of all, Amy felt bad that Nethra was having such a hard time. She wanted to send Nethra an email to cheer her up. But it was hard to know what to write. The longer she worried about it, the harder it seemed to find the right words. Then one day at school she saw a poster that had a cat clinging to a branch, using only its front paws. Under the picture it said, "Hang in there." Those three words seemed perfect.

That night Amy sent Nethra a simple email. She wrote, "Hang in there, Nethra. I love you!"

The next day she got an email back from Nethra. "Thanks for writing," she wrote. "It made me feel better. And I am hanging in there!"

## Talk About It

Do you ever have a hard time finding the words to show you care? If so, why do you think it's hard? If not, how do you find the words?

# The New Guy

"I'll take the new guy," Derrek said, pointing at Tyrone. The fourth-grade class looked in Tyrone's direction as he walked toward the side of the field where Derrek's kickball team was gathering.

"What position do you want to play?" Derrek asked Tyrone. Tyrone chose first base. And he played it well. He tagged the first kicker out and made a diving catch to get another out and save a run. After the game was over, Derrek let Tyrone ahead of him in line at the water fountain so he was first.

Derrek did a lot of little things to help Tyrone that day. He showed him where his classes were and told him about the teachers. At lunchtime he found Tyrone sitting alone and asked him to join him at his table.

At the end of the day, the boys walked home together. They discovered they lived on the same block.

"See you tomorrow," Tyrone called out as he opened his front door.

"Bye, Tyrone," Derrek said.

"You can call me Ty. That's what my friends call me."

## Talk About It

What did Derrek do to make Tyrone feel more comfortable at his new school? Why do you think Derrek did these things? What happened as a result?

# The Spider Project

Everyone in the fifth grade thought Mary Jo was cute. But when Jeanice first met her, Mary Jo would hardly speak—so Jeanice assumed she was stuck up.

Then the girls were assigned to work on a science project together. Jeanice wanted to do a project on spiders. She loved the outdoors and looked forward to spending afternoons outside photographing and studying spiders. When Mary Jo said she couldn't be in the sun for very long, Jeanice thought she was afraid of spiders but was embarassed to admit it. But Mary Jo said she would be happy to do research on the Internet about the spiders Jeanice photographed.

During the next few weeks, Jeanice began to know Mary Jo better. She learned that Mary Jo's long hair was a wig. Mary Jo lost her hair when she had chemotherapy. Last summer, Mary Jo was very sick and was still in the process of getting better. Her quiet way was not because Mary Jo was a snob. It was because she didn't feel well much of the time.

Mary Jo missed a lot of school that fall. But she didn't get behind in her studies because Jeanice took the homework assignments to her and explained the lessons she missed. Jeanice cared a lot about her new friend and was glad she could help her with school stuff.

## Talk About It

In what ways did Jeanice change in this story? Why did those changes happen? How did she show she cared? Tell about a time you misjudged someone.

# Dodgeball

Wynona's dodgeball team had a chance to win the game. All but one of the kids on the other team were out. Wynona's teammate Mason had the ball. If he hit the other team's last remaining player, his team would win. If he missed, they'd lose. Mason threw the ball, but it skipped past the boy in the square and out of bounds. "Ha!" shouted the boy. "We win!"

"Aw, man!" said another one of Wynona's teammates. "You should have let me take the last shot. I would've hit him!"

"Yeah!" said a girl. "Mason can't throw. Everyone knows that."

Mason hung his head in embarrassment and walked slowly away from the dodgeball square.

"Hey, you guys," Wynona said. "Give him a break." Then she caught up with Mason. "Don't worry about them," she said as they walked.

"Well, they're right. I did lose the game for us," Mason said.

"No way," Wynona said. "We had lots of chances to win—that was only one of them. Besides, it's just a game. It's supposed to be fun."

Mason smiled. "Yeah, I guess you're right."

## Talk About It

What does it mean to be a "good sport"? What does being a good sport have to do with caring?

# Cheerfulness

Being cheerful means showing happiness. You show that you are in a good mood. You get excited about things to come, and you believe things will turn out well. You like to laugh and smile. Some people call being cheerful being "sunny." And like a sunny day, this trait "shines" on everyone you meet, making them happier, too.

# A New Attitude

Saturday morning is when Sanjay and his dad clean the apartment. Some chores are just plain gross to Sanjay—like cleaning the bathroom. One weekend, he was complaining noisily about it. "This just stinks!" he said.

"Sanjay," his dad said, "can you think of any way to make this job more pleasant?"

"The only way I could make it more pleasant is to watch someone else do it," Sanjay replied.

"You're spending about 52 hours a year in a grumpy mood because of your attitude about this chore," Dad said. "You *do* have a choice about it."

Sanjay smiled as he imagined a housekeeper coming to do this chore for him, but he quickly came back to reality. A housekeeper was not the kind of choice his dad meant.

The wheels of Sanjay's mind began to turn. "Maybe if I put on some loud music, I'll be in a better mood," he said.

"I bet that would help me, too, while I mop the kitchen floor," his dad said.

In no time at all, they were singing with the music as they worked. Sanjay laughed as he caught a glimpse of his dad dancing with the mop in the kitchen.

## Talk About It

What do you do to make chores and other responsibilities more enjoyable? What are some other ideas you could try?

# The Boys' Room

It was Emily's first day at her new school and she was really nervous. She wanted to do everything right, so she could blend in with her new classmates.

Already, though, the day had started off wrong because she arrived late. Since she was tardy anyway, she decided to go to the restroom to fix her hair before going to class. As Emily looked in the mirror, something strange caught her eye. It was a urinal on the wall. "Oh, no!" she said. "I'm in the boy's bathroom!"

Embarrassed, Emily ran for the door. She couldn't get out fast enough! But just as she was exiting the restroom she ran right into two boys in the doorway. The boys looked at each other and cracked up laughing. *Yikes*, thought Emily, running down the hall. This was the kind of embarrassment that made a person want to curl up in bed and not come out for a year. She usually had a great sense of humor, but it was not working today. Even on the bus ride home she could still see the surprised look on the boys' faces and hear their giggles.

A few weeks later, Emily shared this story with a couple of her new friends and they squealed with laughter. Emily found that she was able to laugh, too. She realized it wasn't such a big deal after all.

## Talk About It

Why do you think Emily's sense of humor was "not working" at first? Were you ever able to laugh at yourself when you goofed up? Tell about it. How did it feel?

# The Basement Job

Logan and his mom ran out to greet Rodney and help him bring his duffle bag inside. Rodney was grinning from ear to ear. He was excited to be spending the night with his friend. He hadn't seen Logan all summer, since Rodney started helping his dad finish their basement.

During dinner, Logan's mom asked Rodney how he was enjoying his summer. "You seem pretty happy," she said. "Isn't it hard to be working so much when your friends are out playing?"

"I am happy," Rodney replied. "Working in the basement may not sound fun, but it's not bad. And I like working with my dad." He paused for a minute to think. Then he said, "Sometimes it's frustrating not seeing my friends as much. But I'm really excited about the new rec room. Looking forward to that helps."

"I'm looking forward to that rec room, too," Logan said. "Then we can hang out all the time."

"And we'll have a cool new place to do it," Rodney said.

## Talk About It

Describe a time when you found a way to be happy even though you were doing something hard or boring. What did you do to make it more fun?

# In the Art Room

Debbie beamed a big smile when she saw Natasha come into the art room. They were best friends and they both looked forward to the weekly art class they took together. But today Natasha didn't return Debbie's smile. She was steaming as she sat down next to Debbie. A girl had called her a name at recess, and she was furious.

"Cheer up," Debbie said. "Who cares what that girl thinks?"

"I don't feel like cheering up right now," Natasha said.

A little later, Debbie lightly tapped Natasha's arm and made a goofy face. Debbie laughed, but Natasha didn't.

Debbie then drew a couple of funny cartoon faces and showed them to Natasha. Natasha only gave a fake smile.

When Debbie started humming a silly tune, her friend finally broke down and cracked a smile. Then both girls laughed and laughed. It was very hard for them to get quiet when the teacher came into the room. They held their breath and their faces turned red. Finally they calmed down.

As soon as class was over, they looked at each other and burst out laughing again.

## Talk About It

What do you do to cheer up someone you care about? How does it feel when you try but you can't cheer the person up? What do you do to stay cheerful even when someone around you isn't?

# 500 Laughs

Dominic chewed on a handful of dried-apricot-and-nut mix. "Do apricots come from Aprica?" he asked, holding up a piece of apricot to look at it closely.

Mom and Dad grinned, but his sister Shandra laughed out loud.

Dominic continued chewing, wondering what was so funny. Shandra informed him that there was a continent named Africa, but not "aprica." Then Mom said, "You know, Shandra, you used to call furniture *furnichair*." Shandra and her brother both laughed at that, and so did Mom and Dad.

"Listen to this," Dad said, pointing at his news magazine.

"Somebody has actually calculated how many times a day children laugh. Can you guess what it is?"

"A hundred!" Dominic said.

"Close," Dad said. "Actually, most children laugh about 500 times a day!"

"I'm not sure I laugh that much in a year," Mom said.

"Oh, sure you do," Dad said. "It's usually the kids who get us laughing."

Shandra grabbed her brother's hand, and they took a bow in front of Mom and Dad. "Presenting Shandra and Dominic—child comedians!" she said grandly.

## Talk About It

Is laughter important in your life? Why or why not? How many times a day do you think you laugh? Who makes you laugh the most?

# Citizenship

You are a citizen of many communities—your class-room, your school, your neighborhood, your town, your state, your country—even the world! Showing good citizenship means being a good citizen. Good citizens are proud of their communities and do things to make them better. They also obey the rules of all their communities, from classroom rules to the laws of their country.

# The Walkathon

It was the Monday after the walkathon, and Danny felt great—and a little sad. He had been the student in charge of this project at his school, and his classmates raised over $1,000 for the school's new media center. His group spent many hours signing up volunteers to walk, making banners, and collecting donations. The event was a huge success. But now that it was all over he would miss working on such an important cause with friends and classmates. It had given him a lot of energy and pride.

After school, Danny pulled on his backpack and ran to meet his friends from the walkathon on the playground. Everyone was still buzzing about their month of work on the project. They all agreed with Danny. They'd miss working together to help their school. As they sat on the monkey bars, they recalled many of the fun times they had working on the walkathon.

"Hey," Danny said, jumping from the bars to face his friends. "Why don't we keep getting together? There are plenty of things that need doing around here."

"That's a great idea," one of his friends said. "We're a team now." Everyone agreed, and they began to plan their next project.

## Talk About It

Why do Danny and his friends want to do another project together? What are some things you can do to improve your school community?

# Crying at the Parade

Ruth stood on the sidewalk watching the parade. A high school band marched past playing exciting, upbeat music. The brass horns gleamed in the sun and the percussionists smiled as they pounded on their drums. When a colorful float and a carload of people waving flags drove by, tears welled up in Ruth's eyes. How embarassing! She was crying right in front of everybody.

Her neighbor, Ms. Nelson, tapped her on the shoulder and asked what was wrong.

"I don't know what's wrong," Ruth said. "I always get this way at parades. It makes me want to avoid parades all together. Everyone around me is screaming and cheering—and I'm crying!"

A smile spread across Ms. Nelson's face. "Ruth, I'm the same way," she said. "I always cry at parades."

"You do?" Ruth asked with surprise, as she watched Ms. Nelson dab her own eyes with a tissue.

"Sure," her neighbor said. "There's nothing shameful about our tears. Parades remind us of all that is best about our community and our country. And sometimes, when we're so proud we could burst, we cry instead."

Soldiers carrying huge flags paraded by next, and this time Ruth didn't try to hide her tears.

## Talk About It

What makes you proud of your community or your country? Why?

# Flowers Around the Mailbox

Several kids in Quentin's neighborhood were teaming up to help elderly people clean and fix their homes. Quentin was not excited—extra work didn't sound very fun at all. But his mom really wanted him to help out. So for three weeks, he and the other kids did chores that weren't too hard for them but were tough for the older neighbors: lawn mowing, replacing ceiling light bulbs, hammering down a loose step, and painting a cupboard door.

As Quentin did more chores and got to know more of his neighbors, he began to enjoy the work. He loved doing the yard work best of all. As he looked at the neatly trimmed shrubs and smelled Mrs. Smith's freshly mowed lawn, he felt great about his contribution to the neighborhood. He took a big bag of weeds to the garbage dumpster and met Mrs. Smith on his way back to the house. "May I bring some flowers from home and plant them around your mailbox?" he asked her.

"Why, of course, Quentin," she replied, smiling kindly. "They'll be a nice treat every time I get the mail."

Quentin had a lot of fun hanging out with the other kids and helping people who needed it. Their work made a big difference in the neighborhood, and it felt good to see how grateful the elderly neighbors were.

## Talk About It

Do you think Quentin is correct to think their work made a big difference? Why or why not? In what ways do you or people you know contribute to your neighborhood? What are some other ways you could contribute?

# Election Day

Billy's school was getting ready for a mock presidential election. Students would get to cast a vote for the candidate they thought would be the best president. Billy's fifth-grade class was in charge of preparing for the election. They built voting booths, made ballots, hung posters, and arranged voting times for every class.

At first, Billy didn't like the idea. "It's silly to do all this work for an election that doesn't even count," he said to his buddies.

In the weeks before the election, Billy's class studied the rights and privileges that citizens have. He thought it was cool that, when he was older, his vote would help choose the leader of his country—as well as other important leaders, like governors, senators, and city council members. All these people made important decisions about the communities Billy belonged to, like his country, his state, his town . . . even his local library system.

On voting day, Billy and his classmates set up voting booths along the walls in the cafeteria. They hung posters decorated in red, white, and blue announcing the election. Billy helped keep the polling area orderly and answered questions other kids had. When he looked around the cafeteria and thought about all the work he and his class had done, he felt proud. When he overheard some kids making fun of the mock election, he remembered he sounded like that a couple weeks ago. But after being involved in the process, he realized he enjoyed it.

## Talk About It

Why didn't Billy like the idea of the mock election at first? Why do you think he ended up enjoying it? What changed his mind?

# A Cornucopia Contribution

LaDonna climbed out of the pool, dripping water into a puddle as she dried off on the concrete deck. She loved swimming in the YWCA's indoor heated pool during the fall, when it was cool and windy outside, and she went almost every Saturday morning. It was only one block from her apartment. She also took gymnastics and computer classes at the Y. It was one of her favorite places.

LaDonna dressed in the locker room and got ready to walk home. As she was passing through the lobby, the activities director called out to her. "LaDonna, do you have a minute?" Ms. Lewis asked.

LaDonna sat in a plastic chair in Ms. Lewis' office, and the director sat on her desk. "Autumn is coming," the director said. "I was wondering if you would decorate the bulletin board in the lobby for the new season."

LaDonna didn't know what to say. She would love to do anything Ms. Lewis asked her, but she didn't think she was very good at art. She didn't want to make an ugly bulletin board for everyone to see. Finally she said, "I'm not very good at crafts and stuff. I think you should get somebody else to do it."

"I think you're just the person for the job," Ms. Lewis said. "You love our Y, and you're an important part of this community. You come here every week."

"I don't know," LaDonna said. "It won't look good if I do it."

"It will look fine, LaDonna. I'll tell you what—I'll help you."

continued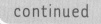

# A Cornucopia Contribution (continued)

Those were the magic words. LaDonna felt she could do it if Ms. Lewis helped, and she was excited to do a project with someone she admired. She called her mom and asked if she could stay later. Then she and Ms. Lewis cut out a pattern for a large cornucopia. They cut out beautiful fruits and red-and-green vegetables to fill the basket. LaDonna traced colorful letters from stencils and she spelled out GIVE THANKS on the board.

## Talk About It

Why did Ms. Lewis pick LaDonna to help her? Why did LaDonna decide to do it even though she didn't think she was good at art?

# Cleanliness

Cleanliness means keeping things neat and clean. You do things like brush your teeth, bathe, and comb your hair to keep your body clean. You might be responsible for cleaning chores at home, classroom jobs, or keeping a desk or locker neat. When you value cleanliness, you show respect for people, property, and the planet.

# High-Speed Germs

Ray drew circles on a piece of paper as Mr. Jacobs from Clean Care gave a presentation to the class on hygiene. Mr. Jacobs visited Ray's class every year since kindergarten and Ray was bored. *Bo-o-o-o-o-o-ring!* he thought. Mr. Jacobs pointed to hygiene rules on a poster, and Ray put his head down. *I've heard this speech so many times, I could give it myself,* he thought.

Then Mr. Jacobs said something that caught Ray's attention. "The spray from a sneeze can travel up to 25 feet. And it moves at 100 miles an hour!"

Ray looked up. "Oh, gross!" he said out loud before he caught himself. His classmates looked at him and laughed. Ray's mind was racing. "A hundred miles an hour? Whoa! And 25 feet is almost as wide as the classroom."

"Yes, it is gross," said Mr. Jacobs, smiling. "Imagine all those high-speed germs flying toward you. That's why it's so important to cover your nose and mouth when you sneeze. To prevent the spread of colds and flu."

Mr. Jacobs kept talking about how to prevent colds and flu, only now he had Ray's attention. When the bell rang, Mr. Jacobs passed out small boxes of tissue and little dispensers of hand cleanser. Ray took one of each.

## Talk About It

Besides covering your nose and mouth when you sneeze, what are some other rules of good hygiene? Why are these rules important?

# Clean at School

"Take out your spelling workbooks," said Mr. Austin. "Let's review this week's lesson."

Isabel rummaged through her desk, but she couldn't find her workbook. Here was her math workbook and here was a magazine, but no spelling book. She pulled out a pack of tissues, some *used* tissues, a pen and four pencils, an eraser, some wadded up old assignments, a smooshed sandwich in a baggie, some coins, chapstick, two CDs, sunglasses, one flip-flop, a movie ticket stub, a notebook, and her favorite fishing cap.

"Hey, I've been looking for this," she said, holding up the cap. Some kids laughed, but Mr. Austin didn't. "Here it is," Isabel said finally, pulling out the spelling book.

At recess that afternoon, Isabel was talking to her friend Jaffar on the playground. Jaffar was a friend, but also *more* than a friend. She liked him a lot.

"Isabel, you sure are messy," he said, laughing.

Isabel laughed, too, but quickly asked if Jaffar had seen their favorite TV show last night. The reason she changed the subject so fast was because she was embarassed. She didn't mind having a messy desk—that was her own business, wasn't it? But she didn't want anyone to think she was a slob. She *especially* didn't want Jaffar to think so.

## Talk About It

Is it anyone else's business how Isabel keeps her desk? Why or why not? Should she change the way she keeps it? What are some problems that could occur if Isabel does not clean out her desk?

# The Closet Clean-up

When Ellen went to the closet to find her umbrella, she found dust, old magazines, shoes, and a pile of clothes—but no umbrella. Not yet, anyway. She and her older sister Alyssa were planning to take a walk in the rain, but when they couldn't find umbrellas they decided to clean out their closet instead.

They both found clothes that didn't fit anymore. Ellen tried to squeeze into her favorite jeans, but she couldn't do it comfortably. Once she had them on she could hardly breathe!

"Time to give those up," Alyssa told her sister.

"But they're my favorites!" Ellen protested.

"Maybe you should take a look in the mirror," Alyssa said. When Ellen saw how silly she looked with the jeans so high above her ankles, the girls burst out laughing. She couldn't get them off fast enough.

There also was no reason to keep all those old magazines. "Make a pile for recycling," Alyssa said. After the closet was empty, they dusted the shelf and vacuumed the floor. And they found the umbrella. It had been hidden behind an empty cardboard box. Finally, the girls put their clothes and a few toys back into the closet. It wasn't only neater, but it seemed a lot bigger.

"That was actually kind of fun," Ellen said.

## Talk About It

Why do you think Ellen thought the closet clean-up was fun? How do you think the closet got so messy in the first place? What could Ellen and Alyssa do to make sure it doesn't get that messy again?

# The Highway Crew

Tina, her brother Jack, and their dad put on their orange vests and walked over to join the rest of the volunteers. They had signed up to clean a section of a local highway. After they listened to the crew leader explain the safety rules, they put on gloves, grabbed some plastic bags, and headed out to work.

Tina picked up a soggy old sock and dropped it into her bag. Then she collected some rusty cans and empty cigarette packs. "Gross!" she said.

"No kidding," said Jack. "This highway is disgusting." They worked for several hours, filling bag after bag with bottles, food wrappers, moldy newspapers, old shoes, batteries, scratched CDs . . . even a ripped-up teddy bear. They tightly secured each bag with a tie and left them all under a bridge to be picked up by the sanitation department.

After the clean-up, Tina, Jack, and their dad drove past the area they had just worked on. "There's not a speck of trash," Tina said. "The grass looks so pretty."

## Talk About It

What are some areas in your community that often are littered? What can you do about? Why do some people litter, while others don't?

# Breathing Better

G abe had asthma. That's what the nurse at the clinic called it. Before she told him what it was, he thought everybody had trouble breathing sometimes.

Besides giving his trouble a name, the nurse also helped Gabe figure out what things triggered the asthma. Some people react to cats or dogs, some to bubble bath, while others to dust or mold.

*Uh-oh*, Gabe thought. *Leonard's and my room could be a real trouble spot.*

When he and his mom got home from the clinic, they went straight to the bedroom. Not only was the furniture dusty, but so was the open window sill. And Leonard had an old slice of pizza under the bed and a half-eaten apple molding in the trash can. Gabe began to wheeze as he looked at his room and had to use his new inhaler.

"Leonard," Gabe said. "I have to get out of here. If you'll clean our room, I'll do our laundry on Saturday."

"Anything to keep us out of the emergency room," Leonard laughed, but Gabe knew he was glad to help.

After that, Gabe dusted and vacuumed their room every week. And Leonard threw leftover food in the kitchen trash. Their mom bought special bed sheets and a carpet spray, too. By learning about his asthma and how it worked, Gabe helped control it. It felt really good to take charge that way. And his room was a nicer place to be, too.

## Talk About It

Keeping a clean room helped Gabe control his asthma. What other benefits are there to keeping your room and other personal spaces clean?

# Compassion

When you have compassion you feel bad for a person or animal who is suffering or hurt. When others go through hard times, you show you care by helping them if you can or by just listening to them.

# The Teddy Bear Note

Katrina carefully opened the little envelope she found tucked into the pouch of her book bag. Inside was a note written on green stationery, decorated with small teddy bears.

"Dear Katrina," the note began. "Thanks for inviting me to your birthday party. I had a great time. I'm sorry I didn't get you a present. Love, Rebecca." Under her name, Rebecca had drawn ten little hearts.

Katrina remembered how embarassed Rebecca seemed at the party when Katrina was opening presents. She knew Rebecca's dad had been laid off from his job. She probably couldn't afford to buy a gift. One of the other girls asked Rebecca where her gift was—and Rebecca turned bright red when she did.

Katrina ran to the family desk and got out a sheet of paper. "Dear Rebecca," she wrote. "Thank you for the most special gift of all—your friendship. I know it will last longer than any present."

Then she carefully sealed the envelope, addressed it, put a stamp on it, and ran out to the mailbox to mail it.

## Talk About It

How do you think Katrina felt when she read the note from Rebecca? Why did she write a note back to Rebecca? Have you ever written or received such a note? If so, why?

# Opening Up

Connie and Maria walked home from the rec center together, just like they did every Wednesday afternoon after their acting class. They usually practiced their lines on the way home, but Maria didn't want to today.

"Don't feel bad about forgetting your lines at rehearsal today," Connie said. "You heard what Miss Rainbow told us. Even the best actors mess up sometimes."

Maria did not reply. She was biting her lip to hold back tears.

After walking another block in silence, Connie said, "Talk to me. What's going on?"

It was like the floodgates opened. Flubbing her lines had bothered Maria a little, but something else was bothering her, too. Her aunt and cousins were having some work done on their home and would be staying at Maria's home for a while. The place was going to be very crowded with those rowdy boys around, and Maria was worried about losing her privacy. When she complained about it to her mom, her mom got angry and they had a big fight. Maria knew offering her cousins a place to stay was the right thing to do, and she felt selfish for complaining, but she still was worried about it.

"I understand," Connie said. "No wonder you're upset." Other than that, she just listened. And as they got closer to their block, Maria seemed to be feeling better.

## Talk About It

Do you think talking to Connie made Maria feel better? Why or why not? Connie mainly just listened—should she have done more? Why or why not? Tell about a time you felt better after talking to a friend.

# Summer Job

School had been out a couple days, and the summer stretched out ahead of Sam as he lay in bed and looked out the window. He wondered what he'd do over his vacation.

At breakfast, his dad told Sam about the story he was reading in the newspaper. "Many people are homeless in this area. Whole families are without food and places to stay."

Sam imagined how he would feel if he didn't have a bed or the breakfast in front of him. He looked at his couch and TV and imagined sleeping outside in a park, begging for money or food from strangers. It bothered him so much he decided to find out what he could do. After getting permission from his dad, he looked up the phone numbers of shelters and churches, then began making calls to see if he could help. On his third call, he found a shelter that served meals every day. They needed somebody to help clear tables.

Sam took the volunteer job. Twice a week his dad took him to the shelter and they both worked. Sam liked the responsibility and he liked the people. Before when he saw homeless people he'd just ignore them. But now he saw up close how hard it was for them. It felt good knowing he was helping.

## Talk About It

Do you volunteer to help others in your community? If so, what do you do and why? Why is volunteering a good way to learn about compassion?

# Homesick

Ginger had a great day hiking and fishing with her friend Rene and her family. They grilled hot dogs and roasted marshmallows by the fire that evening. Ginger loved staring into the leaping orange flames while the forest grew dark around them.

But when it was time to go to bed, things changed. Ginger was homesick and couldn't fall asleep on her first night camping. She began to cry quietly.

Rene shined a flashlight on the tent ceiling and rolled over to face her friend. "It's okay," she said. "My mom and dad and I are all here."

"I wish I had Smiley, my teddy," Ginger said.

Rene rolled up a soft T-shirt and tucked it into Ginger's arm. "Close your eyes and pretend this is Smiley."

"Oh, that's silly," Ginger said, but she smiled a little.

"Just try it," said Rene. So Ginger hugged the T-shirt tightly. "Imagine that you're in your own bed at home. You're comfortable and safe."

Ginger began to breathe more easily. The crying grew softer, then stopped. Soon she fell into a peaceful sleep.

## Talk About It

Describe a time you tried to make someone feel less lonely, worried, or scared. How did it go? What about a time someone helped *you* feel less lonely, worried, or scared?

# Tears at the Table

On Friday night, Terry and Ken went out for pizza with their dads and Ken's sister. When Terry and Ken finished eating, they went to play video games while the dads went over some papers they'd brought. They were drawing diagrams for a project they were doing together.

"Can I go with you guys?" Ken's sister Donna asked.

"No way," said Ken. "No girls."

A few minutes later the boys heard Ken's dad shout, "Oh, no! The drawings!" Ken and Terry ran back to the table to see what happened. Donna accidentally had spilled her milk all over the diagrams.

Tears ran down Donna's face as she felt everybody's eyes on her. "I'm sorry!" she bawled. The restaurant became very quiet.

Her dad felt terrible. "Donna, I'm sorry I yelled," he said, helping her clean up the mess. "It's no big deal."

Donna kept crying. "But I ruined your papers," she said.

"It's okay, sweetie," he said. "I'll redraw them."

After the mess was cleaned up and everyone had settled down, Terry said to Donna, "They have a cool video game you might like. Do you want to play?"

Donna looked up at her big brother's friend. "Okay," she said, smiling.

## Talk About It

Why do you think Terry asked Donna to play? How do you think Donna felt? Why?

# Cooperation

Cooperation means being willing to work with other people to get something done. When you cooperate, you're part of a team. You listen to other people's ideas and you don't always have to be the leader or always be right. Most big jobs, and a lot of small ones, require cooperation. Being able to cooperate can make life easier and more fun. Cooperating can also help you accomplish more.

# Dinner Duties

Shantell's mom and dad had invited some friends over for dinner. Before the guests arrived, Mom sat down with Shantell and her sisters to talk about the evening. "This will be fun tonight, but I'll need some help from you, okay?"

"Okay, Mom," said Shantell. "What do you need?"

"Well, I'll need some help keeping the dog under control when our friends first get here. You know how Dante likes to jump up on people. And after dinner, would you guys do the dishes so us grown-ups can talk?"

The girls nodded their heads. They could do that.

"Great, thank you. And there's one more thing," said their mom. "I'd like you to be on your best behavior all night. What do you think I mean by that?"

"Not being wild," said Tia.

"Being polite," said Shantell.

"Not always asking for attention," Fatimah added.

"Mom, can I still tell my jokes?" Shantell asked. She was famous for her silly puns. She loved making people laugh, especially the grown-ups who came to their parents' parties. They usually thought she was especially funny.

"Of course," Mom said. "I'm not asking you not to be yourself. I'm asking you to cooperate."

## Talk About It

What are some other examples of times adults ask kids for their cooperation? Do kids ever need adults to cooperate? If so, what are some examples?

# The Squishy Banana

When James and Richard came home from school they were both starving. Richard ran to the fruit bowl and grabbed the last piece of fruit—a big, ripe banana.

"Hey," said James. "I'm hungry, too."

And the boys began to tug on the banana.

"Wait," Richard said. "This banana's going to be bruised and squishy. Let's figure out how to solve this without a fight."

James agreed that would be best, and the boys talked about some solutions. They thought about cutting it in half, but they were both too hungry for that. James suggested they bike to the convenience store to buy another banana, but they didn't want to wait. Richard suggested they make a peanut butter and banana sandwich and split it. That would be enough for both of them. But a sandwich didn't sound good to James. Then they looked in the cabinet and found a package of instant banana pudding. This was the perfect solution.

"Let's make this," Richard said, reading the pudding box.

James found the mixer and dumped the pudding mix into the bowl. He measured the milk and added it while Richard sliced the banana. Soon the boys were eating pudding with sliced bananas on top.

## Talk About It

Is it easier or harder to cooperate with a good friend or sibling than it is with someone you don't know as well? Why?

# Scrapbook Group

Kareem's teacher told the class about the new social studies assignment. She divided everyone into groups of three to make a scrapbook on a country of their choice. "Groups will meet for the first time today," Ms. Navin said. "By the end of class you need to know what country you're doing and each group member's job."

When Kareem's group met, Kim took charge. "We'll do Denmark," she said, before anyone else had a chance to make a suggestion. "And my dad has a wood shop so I'll have him help me cut out an outline of the country in thin plywood. We'll glue that on the cover of our scrapbook."

"I guess that's okay," Marlee said.

Kim kept talking: "I'll research Denmark's culture—like what they eat and what they do for fun. You collect information on history and geography, okay, Marlee? Then you can make a map. And Kareem, you research the economy."

"I want to research culture," Marlee said.

"You're doing history and geography," Kim told her.

"I'd rather research the kids," Kareem said. "I want to find out what games kids play, what chores they do, and what school is like."

"No," said Kim. "You're doing economy."

Ms. Navin said, "Five minutes to go, class."

Marlee put her head down on the desk and tuned out. Kareem groaned to himself. *Who made Kim the boss?* he thought.

## Talk About It

Can you find any examples of cooperation in this story? If so, what are they? What can Kareem and the others do in the next five minutes to make the project go better? Be specific.

# The Secret Club

Naveeta and her friends formed a club, but it broke up after the first meeting. Everyone in the club wanted to be the president. When nobody would give in, they all got mad and went home.

A few days later the subject of the club came up again while Naveeta and the others were having lunch at school.

"I've been thinking about the club," Brook said between bites of her sandwich.

"Yeah, I have, too," Naveeta said. "I really want it to work."

"I have a solution to the president problem," Brook continued. "We can take turns being president. We'll draw straws to see who goes first."

"Great idea," Jill and Lan chimed in.

"You can take me out of the running," Naveeta said. "I want to be secretary. Last night Dad gave me one of his extra appointment calendars. I think it will be fun to schedule the meetings and take notes."

"Hold up!" said Lan. "What if I want to be the secretary?"

They all laughed, but they knew this time trouble cooperating would not end their club. They wanted it too much. The girls kept eating, and by the end of lunch they'd thought up a secret name and handshake for the club.

## Talk About It

Why do you think the girls got so mad over who would be club president? Do you think it will be hard for them to keep cooperating? Explain your answer.

# Cooperative Cooking

Autumn and Cathy swung the double ropes. Nicole stared at the ropes as they beat out their rhythm on the asphalt. She took a deep breath, ran in, and began jumping.

"One, two, three, four! Jump those ropes and jump some more," the girls sang out. Nicole jumped and jumped until she was out of breath, then she jumped out.

"I have to go now," she said.

"Oh, come on," her friends begged. "Jump some more."

"I have to cook," she replied. "Some family friends are coming over tonight and I'm making spinach puff for dinner."

"Let us help you," Autumn said.

"Great idea!" replied Nicole. "That'll be fun."

The girls followed Nicole inside and to the kitchen. She got out the spinach, eggs, cheese, and butter. Cathy chopped the butter while Autumn beat the eggs and added the grated cheese. In a jiffy the ingredients were mixed and ready to pour into the casserole dish. Working together on this project was so much fun, they didn't even complain about cleaning up the kitchen. When the last dish was washed, the girls raced outside to jump rope some more.

## Talk About It

Do you think Autumn and Cathy would have rather stayed outside and kept playing instead of helping Nicole? If so, why do you think they helped her? What would you have done? Why?

# Courage

Having courage means being brave. It takes courage to do something that's difficult or scary. Courage does not mean having no fear; it means having the strength to face a hard or scary situation even though you are afraid.

# Swimming Lessons

**B**rad was in third grade and didn't know how to swim. He and his dad just moved into a building with a swimming pool, and his dad thought it was time for him to learn. So he signed up Brad for swimming lessons at the community center. When they arrived for the first lesson, Brad got scared. "I don't want to," he said. He had heard stories about how you have to jump in and put your head under water. He was afraid he would lose his breath.

"You'll be safe," his dad promised. "The teacher is a pro. There's a lifeguard here, too. And I'll be right up there." He pointed to the bleachers where he'd be sitting.

Brad was still scared, but he nodded his head and let his dad drop him off with the teacher. Bright sun reflected off the surface of the pool as Brad stared into the blue water. His heart was thumping hard.

Dad sat in the bleachers and watched, just like he said he would. Brad did everything the teacher asked—even jumping into the water, where the teacher caught him—and getting his head wet. It wasn't so bad once he did it! After the lesson, Brad got out of the pool. He shook all over from being excited and cold.

"Can we stay longer, Dad?" he asked. "Maybe you could catch me when I jump in."

## Talk About It

Describe a time you were scared to try something new. Why were you scared? How did it turn out?

# Just Our Imagination

Glenda and Tonya's dad was always home when the girls got home from school, but today he had a meeting and was going to be late. He thought the girls were old enough to be alone for an hour until he got there. Glenda was 12 and very responsible. Tonya was only 9, but her sister always watched out for her.

Dad covered all the safety rules with them the night before. The most important one was not to let anyone inside.

The girls had fun when they first got home. They played cards and watched TV. It felt grown up to stay home alone, but after a while they got a little restless and wanted to go outside. They heard their friends gathering in the alley to play, and all they could do was stand by the window and watch.

"Come on out," the kids yelled, waving them outside.

They shook their heads and mouthed "We can't."

Just then the girls heard a loud bang. They jumped. "Who's at the door?" Tonya asked. Glenda saw that her sister was scared.

"I bet it's one of those kids wanting us to come outside," Glenda replied. She tried to show Tonya that she was not afraid so she'd calm down. The two went toward the door to look through the peep hole. Their hearts raced when they heard the bang again. This time they thought it came from inside the house!

"Maybe it's a burglar or a kidnapper!" Tonya whispered.

continued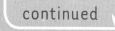

## Just Our Imagination (continued)

"Quit scaring yourself," Glenda said. "I'll call Dad." But as she picked up the phone, they heard another sound—hissing. Both girls sighed in relief to realize the knocking had come from the radiator.

When their dad arrived home, the girls told their father all about their afternoon.

"It was still a little scary," Glenda admitted. "But now I know we were scaring ourselves more than anything."

"You two did great," Dad said, hugging one girl with each arm.

### Talk About It

Talk about a time you let your imagination scare you. Were you able to calm yourself down? If so, how? If not, why not?

# The Tree and the Pond

"C'mon, Musa," said Kevin. "I know your mom said you can't jump off the tree into the pond. But she's not here, so she'll never know you did it. I can't believe you won't do it! You're such a chicken."

Musa looked away angrily. The two boys sat on the shore of the green pond. They couldn't see the bottom, and his mom had told him it wasn't safe to jump there. It made him mad that his friend was pressuring him so much.

"Your mom's too strict," Kevin taunted. "I think I need some friends who aren't scared of their mommies."

"I'm not jumping off that tree," Musa said. He threw a rock into the water and watched it splash.

"You're a chicken," Kevin said, and made a chicken noise. "Boc boc boc!"

"Kevin, I'm not going to do it. My mom trusts me. And I don't think it's safe." Musa stood up and looked down at Kevin. "This isn't fun to me, so I'm going home." Musa felt as if a million-pound weight had been lifted off his shoulders as he walked away.

## Talk About It

Why was Musa so mad at Kevin for pressuring him? Have you ever been in a similar situation? Do you think it would take more courage to do something dangerous like jumping in the pond, or to stand up to a friend's pressure? Why?

# The Speech

A popular children's writer was visiting Luke's school. She wasn't just any author—she was Luke's *favorite* author. He'd read all her books. So when the principal asked for a volunteer to give a short speech to introduce her at the assembly, Luke jumped at the chance.

He planned his introduction carefully, writing it out at the kitchen table. He mentioned her awards, and even wrote a joke. He went over and over the speech in his mind until he knew it well. He was excited for the big day to come. But as the visit got closer, Luke grew nervous. A lot of people would be watching him.

When he told his sister how nervous he was, Carolyn suggested he say the introduction aloud a few times. "You could even practice once or twice with me as your audience," she said. "Then you'll be comfortable saying it in front of people."

Luke thought that was a good idea. Carolyn sat on her bed and listened quietly as he gave the speech, and she even laughed at his joke.

Two days later the author came to school. When Luke introduced her to the school, he was confident. He knew his speech so well he was only a little nervous. A lot of faces stared up at him. But everything turned out fine. The kids laughed at his joke, and so did the author! When she came to the stage, she thanked Luke for the nice introduction. Later, Luke thanked his sister. "Your idea really helped," he said. "Thanks a lot."

## Talk About It

Why do you think it can be scary to speak or perform in front of an audience? What can you do to help make it less scary?

# Bracing for Headgear

Angelina needed braces. She had "braced herself" for this. She even convinced herself that braces were cool. Lots of kids in her class had them. So when she went to the orthodontist's office, she was even a little excited.

Then Dr. Samson dropped a bombshell. "Angelina," she said, "I'd like you to wear headgear."

Angelina's heart stopped. "What does it look like?" she asked. Dr. Samson showed her. It was a piece of wire that went from her teeth around her head. A pad stretched across the back. "Oh, it's so ugly," Angelina said sadly. She was sure kids at school would make fun of her if she wore that thing to school.

"It will really help you," the doctor said. "And it will shorten the length of time you're in braces."

Angelina gulped. "How long do I have to wear it?" she asked.

"That depends on you," Dr. Samson said. "Usually more than a year— if you wear it only at night. But one girl wore it day and night, and was totally out of it in nine months."

Angelina nodded and smiled a little. It made her feel better to know what to expect, and it felt good to hear about someone else going through the same thing.

## Talk About It

Do you think Angelina will wear the headgear to school? Why or why not? What would you do? Why?

# Creativity

When you are creative you like to come up with new ideas or solutions to problems. You use your imagination to think of new possibilities. Creative people like to *create*—to write, paint or draw, sing, play an instrument, build things, make sculptures, and so on. When people think of creative people, inventors and artists often come to mind. But people can be creative in many different ways.

# Knit One, Purl Two

Ling pressed her nose against the window of the yarn shop. The shop appeared about two weeks ago in the store that used to rent videos.

It was really something! The sunlit shelves were overflowing with yarn in more colors than in a giant crayon box. Scarves and caps with pompoms hung on the wall. In a cozy corner, several chairs were drawn together. People were knitting and talking.

Ling put her hand on the door and walked in. She stood back and watched the knitters. "Is knitting hard?" she asked the shopkeeper.

"Oh no," the shopkeeper laughed. "There are only two stitches—knit and purl."

Ling watched the class a while longer and then the shopkeeper invited her to give it a try. She gave Ling some yarn and taught her how to knit and purl. The teenage girl next to Ling helped her when she got stuck.

Ling loved it! No wonder the store seemed to call to her. Knitting felt so good. She loved creating something new from the yarn, even though her creation today wasn't much more than a few wrinkled inches of yarn stitched together. She knew she'd get better if she kept working at it. "Knit one, purl two," she repeated to herself as she walked home. She liked saying the names of the knitting stitches over and over again in different rhythms.

## Talk About It

Why do you think Ling liked knitting so much? Is there a craft or pastime that makes you feel that way? Tell about it.

# The Clay Bowl

Drew hurried to the cafeteria for his after-school program. Today they were making clay pots and he was excited. He went to a long table and joined several others.

Soon a teacher came by and handed each person a piece of wet clay. She showed everyone how to prepare the clay by working the air bubbles out. Drew loved the feel of it squishing between his fingers.

When the clay was ready he slowly stretched it into the shape of a wide bowl. He imagined his mom could keep fruit in his bowl in the kitchen when it was done. When he finished shaping his bowl he put it on the shelf. He couldn't get all the clay out from under his fingernails when he washed his hands, and he couldn't get the smell completely off either. Drew didn't mind, though. He was a clay artist.

The next afternoon Drew painted his creation midnight blue, with yellow suns and moons, then glazed it. After the kids left that night, the teacher put all their pieces in the kiln to fire them. Drew couldn't wait to see it when it was done. It was going to be so cool!

But when Drew picked up his bowl the next afternoon he noticed the rim wasn't quite even all the way around. One side had a crease in it, and one of his yellow moons looked more like a banana. Maybe it wasn't such a cool bowl after all.

Then Drew remembered the fun he had making the bowl, and he changed his mind. *This is beautiful,* he thought, *even if it has a few mistakes.*

## Talk About It

Drew thinks the bowl is beautiful, even though it has mistakes. Have you ever felt the same way about something you created? Are you often hard on yourself and your creations? Why?

# Cooking Dinner

Jazmin and her little brother Andre got children's cookbooks for their birthdays, which were both in spring. One Saturday they asked their mom if they could plan a meal. "We'll make it healthy and balanced," they promised. Their mom agreed, and the two kids quickly began flipping through the books and planning the dinner. Of course there were lots of desserts they wanted to make, but they knew their mom wouldn't let them do more than one.

In the kitchen they whispered ideas to each other, so their mom and dad wouldn't hear. They wanted the dinner to be a surprise. They made a shopping list, and then they called their mom in. "Can you take us to the grocery store?" Jazmin asked.

"Can *we* do the shopping from our *own* grocery list?" added Andre.

"And could we all dress up for dinner?" Jazmin asked.

Their mom looked a little stunned by all the questions, but she smiled. "Yes, yes, and yes," she said.

The afternoon was filled with grocery shopping and cooking. A half hour before dinner was served, Jazmin and Andre handed out menus. They read: FIRST COURSE: spaghetti; SECOND COURSE: coffee (for grown-ups) and hot chocolate (for kids); THIRD COURSE: green bean casserole; FOURTH COURSE: fresh strawberries and whipped cream.

Their mom and dad loved it and asked the kids if they would do it again sometime soon.

## Talk About It

What does cooking have to do with creativity? What other ways can you think of to be creative?

# The Health Bug

Mick and Eileen partnered up to make an entry for the science fair. The first thing they had to do was figure out what their project would be.

"Let's do something on bugs," Mick said. He loved bugs. He studied them, collected them, and drew pictures of them. He liked beautiful bugs, like woolie worms, and ugly bugs, like June bugs, with their neat, plastic-looking shells. When he grew up, he was going to be a scientist.

But Eileen was more interested in health. She wanted to be a doctor when she grew up. "Let's think about this some more," she said.

The next time the two met they started researching bugs and health topics on the Internet and in the encyclopedia. They learned that some bugs, like mosquitos, ticks, fleas, and lice, carry diseases and can infect animals—including humans. "I've got photos of those bugs we could display," Mick said. They decided to go to the library and check out some books to learn more.

That night, Eileen got her mom to help her make a stuffed insect out of terrycloth and cotton. When she showed it to Mick the next day, they named it—and their science fair entry—"The Health Bug." Their project would explain how several different kinds of bugs spread disease, what kinds of disease they spread, and how people can protect themselves. The friends put their heads together and planned the rest of their science fair entry.

## Talk About It

What examples of creativity can you name in this story? Do you think Mick and Eileen have a good partnership? Why? How is it creative?

# The Portrait

Laura was doing her favorite thing—painting a picture. She had been working on this picture, a portrait of her grandfather, for weeks. She mixed some gray into the blotch of white on her pallet so it wasn't so bright. Then she added a couple strokes to the mane of the stallion her grandfather was riding. Its front legs reared into the air.

Laura was proud of Grandpa Jess, an important Chippewa Indian leader. He was so good at many things, and he taught the neighborhood kids a lot of them—like how to ride horses, how to paint pictures, and even how to play chess. In addition, as the tribal council chief, he had the respect and affection of adults, too. Everyone loved Grandpa Jess.

Laura put the finishing touches on a shiny black hoof. Then she backed up and stared at the picture for a long time. She remembered the day the local kids convinced Grandpa Jess to enter the state rodeo—and he won! Laura hoped that she, too, could win a rodeo some day. Her grandfather had taught her to be a pretty good rider.

Laura was done with the picture. It was magnificent.

## Talk About It

Why was the picture so important to Laura? Do you have any skills that a loved one has taught you? What are they? How did you get started?

# Diligence

Diligence means doing your best and finishing what you begin. If you are diligent, you continue to work on something until it's done and you are happy with it. Diligent people are proud of their work. If you are diligent, others can count on you to work hard at whatever you do.

# Learning to Ollie

"Cool!" Kelly called out when Pedro ollied over the curb. The skateboard seemed to stick to his feet in midair. "How'd you get so good at skateboarding?" she asked.

"Just by watching other kids," Pedro said. "Then I picture myself doing what they do. The older kids' tricks show me what I can do."

"It must take a long time," Kelly said. She was sitting on her skateboard with her arms around her knees.

"It took me a couple weeks of practicing to ollie," Pedro said. "And I'm always practicing new tricks."

"I can tell," Kelly said. "You're getting really good." She had been skating for more than a year, but she hadn't learned any good tricks. She was a little frustrated.

"Do you want me to teach you how to ollie?" Pedro asked.

"Definitely!" Kelly said. He showed her how to position her feet and how to click the skateboard's tail. Kelly watched and watched as Pedro showed her again and again. They met again to practice the next day, and the next day after that. In the evenings she practiced at home. She kept telling herself she could do it, even though she took a few spills. Soon, it all clicked in. She showed off her new skills to Pedro. "Check this out!" she said, as she ollied with ease.

"Nice one!" Pedro called out.

## Talk About It

Describe a time you had to work hard at something in order to learn it. What kept you going at it?

# The Squeaky Saxophone

The bleachers were packed with excited parents and friends watching the sixth-grade band's concert. Music filled the gymnasium, and Ramesh concentrated on playing his alto sax. After the last song, Ramesh was surprised by how loud the crowd cheered. The program was a real success, especially considering the players had only had their instruments for three months. He was pretty sure they only made a few mistakes. Actually, he thought they sounded pretty good.

"Great job!" Ramesh's mom said when he found her outside. "How did you like performing?"

"It's fun," Ramesh said. He held up his sax and looked at it. "I never thought I'd be able to make real songs with this thing."

"What an improvement from the first couple weeks, when you were squeaking up the whole house," his mom laughed. "You were really discouraged."

"I was trying so hard, but I just couldn't make the right sounds."

"I thought you were going to quit," his mom said.

"I'm glad I didn't. Hearing all that clapping tonight made it all worth it."

"I'm glad, too. You worked so hard—I'm proud of you."

## Talk About It

Why do you think Ramesh almost quit the saxophone? Why do you think he stuck with it?

# Volcano Project

Jonathan felt the old feeling creeping up on him again as his teacher, Mr. Patel, assigned a project on Hawaiian volcanoes. How was he going to get this assignment done in just four weeks? He always had trouble turning in big projects on time. And now he had karate lessons two nights a week, so that gave him even less time. He needed a plan.

That day after school Jonathan made a list of all the work he needed to do to finish the project. It started with "Do Internet research" and "Check out books from the library." Further down the list it said things like, "Make volcano poster" and "Outline my report." Jonathan decided to start his research that afternoon, even though he had three whole weeks until the due date. He rode his bike to the library with the project instructions and his list in his backpack. Right away he found some great photos on the Internet, and he started to get really excited about his project. Volcanoes were amazing! As he put his library books in his backpack and rode home, Jonathan made a plan to work on his project for 15 to 30 minutes each day he didn't have karate.

After a few days, Jonathan was in better spirits. He'd finished half the things on his list, and it felt great to cross them out. After another week, he had almost everything done. He'd made the poster, outlined the report, *and* written the first half.

When the due date rolled around, Jonathan was confident he'd done a good job. And he hadn't felt much stress about finishing.

## Talk About It

What helped Jonathan to feel less stress about finishing his project? Tell about a time you planned ahead to handle a large project.

# The Soccer Star

More than anything in the world, Lindsay wanted to be a professional soccer player. She could feel the uniform. She could hear the roar of the crowd. She imagined playing in stadiums all over the world. But sometimes her dream seemed almost too big for her to believe in. After all, she was just a kid.

Lindsay worked hard. She played in a local soccer league, and her team practiced three times a week and played a game once a week. Lindsay wanted to do more than that, though, so she began practicing with her next-door neighbor Thuong. They dribbled a ball around the park, polishing up their passing skills. They also stood far apart and worked on their long kicks. Lindsay practiced when she was alone, too. She taped a target on the garage door and took shots at it everyday. Soon she could place the ball perfectly in any corner she aimed at.

Sometimes all that practice helped Lindsay forget how big her dream was. She didn't know if she was going to be a star or not, but she loved working at it.

## Talk About It

What are your big dreams? What are you doing to work toward them?

# It's a Stretch

Laurel unrolled her bright green mat and sat beside her father. The yoga class began. The first warm-up was done in a sitting position with legs outstretched. The students bent forward slowly and stretched their arms toward their toes. As Laurel held her toes, she remembered the first class, when she could only reach her ankles and her dad couldn't get his hands much below his knees. Now they both could touch their toes. That felt really good.

"Yoga is not a competition," the teacher would say each week. "Everyone progresses at their own pace."

Laurel and her dad had progressed a lot over the year. They practiced the stretching and standing poses several times a week at home. Sticking to a practice routine helped them gain greater flexibility and better balance. Sometimes Laurel would get the giggles when they did the standing poses. Several people, including her, wobbled around a lot at first. She thought the "Mountain Pose" was a good name for that exercise—she could have used a mountain to lean on to keep her balance.

Today the class was working on the "Salute to the Sun" exercise. One part was especially hard for Laurel. Weeks ago she couldn't do it, but today she knew she could. She balanced on one foot and one knee, with her hands on the ground. Then she arched her back and inhaled deeply. She held her breath as she clapped her hands together and raised them

continued

# It's a Stretch (continued)

above her head so they pointed up and behind her. Laurel didn't even wobble as she held the pose.

When Laurel rolled up her mat at the end of class, she was beaming. Both she and her dad completed the "Salute to the Sun" without any trouble. And they felt great.

## Talk About It

Why did finishing the "Salute to the Sun" make Laurel feel so good? Do you think it would have been as satisfying if yoga was easier for her? Why or why not?

# Fairness

Fairness means treating people equally. It means giving everyone what they deserve, holding everyone (including yourself) to the same rules, and respecting everyone—whether you like them or not. All people deserve to be treated fairly.

# The Movie Passes

Murray and Gloria rode their bikes slowly down the sidewalk, chatting about school. "Hey, are you going to the movie Friday?" Gloria asked, jumping off a curb.

"No!" Murray said in a huff. He followed her off the curb. "The bus driver said she'd give the movie passes to people who behave on the bus, but then she said, 'All you boys misbehave!'" Even though Murray was mad, he laughed a little when he imitated the bus driver's voice.

"That's not fair," Gloria said. "You're quiet on the bus. You never stand up or throw things."

"I know," Murray said. "I deserved one of those passes." They rode along for a while, past the library and the post office. They rode down a dirt trail to the creek.

Then Gloria said, "Let's talk to her tomorrow. I'll tell her you're good on the bus."

"It won't help," Murray said. "Bus drivers never listen. They're all mean."

"Careful," Gloria said. "Now *you're* not being fair."

## Talk About It

Has anyone ever treated you like you were part of a group instead of an individual person? If so, how did it make you feel and why? If not, how do you think it would feel? Why?

# After Supper

Perry excused himself after supper and went to the bathroom. He took his time, and when he came back the table was cleared and the dishes were clean. "Perry," his dad said, hanging a dishtowel on the fridge. "We need to talk about this." It was the third time that week he'd disappeared when it was time to do dishes. "You need to do your share of the work around here. It's not fair to me and your brother."

Perry thought about it. His teacher said the same thing earlier that day. When she asked the students to rearrange their desks for group work, Perry was off in a corner telling a funny story to someone. "Perry, you need to do your share," his teacher said.

Everyone said Perry was funny and fun to be around, but lately even his friends were getting frustrated with him. Last Sunday, after they were done painting at Ben's house, Perry got ready to leave before the supplies were put away. "That figures," Ben muttered. "You never help clean up."

Perry decided his dad was right. He wasn't being fair. "I'm sorry, Dad," he said, grabbing the broom. "I'm going to try to do better. And to start, I'll sweep the kitchen."

## Talk About It

What might have happened if Perry didn't decide to try to do better, and instead kept avoiding work?

# Things We Can Do

Ramona didn't think it was fair that some people were homeless and hungry. Lots of people had way more than they needed— why should others suffer? "Mom," she said, "I wish we could change things. They should make a law. Everyone gets a decent place to live and healthy food."

"People have been working to wipe out homelessness and hunger for a long time," her mom answered. "It hasn't happened yet. But there are important things we *can* do."

So Ramona, her sister, mom, and dad donated three big bags of groceries to a local homeless shelter. While they were there, they learned other ways they could help. That summer, the family organized two car washes to raise money for the shelter. They talked to people from their neighborhood and collected donations of soap, sponges, and towels. That fall they organized a huge bake sale and raised even more money.

Then, on Thanksgiving, they had two dinners. One was at the shelter, where they helped serve turkey, dressing, mashed potatoes, and sweet potato pie to the residents. The second was pizza at home, because they were too tired to cook for themselves.

"It still seems unfair that people have to live like that," Ramona said.

"It is," her mom replied. "But our work has made a difference."

## Talk About It

What does Ramona mean when she says it's "unfair" that some people are homeless and hungry? What are some things you can do to work for the kind of fairness she's talking about?

# The Interviews

Michael and his friend Freda worked together on a social studies report. Their topic was the Civil Rights movement of the 1960s, when people in the United States fought for equal rights for African Americans. Freda gathered news stories from that time. Michael interviewed people who had lived then. His parents and adult relatives were in that age range. So was his rabbi.

Michael made a phone call to his Uncle Eli. He had heard about his marching for civil rights. "A lot of discrimination was legal," Uncle Eli told him. "There were laws that kept black people and white people separated." Michael could hardly believe this was true.

When he interviewed his rabbi, he talked about helping register African Americans to vote. "It was scary," he told Michael. "Some people would hurt you for helping a black person. But I just had to do it because it was only fair."

After they'd gathered the news stories and finished the interviews, Michael and Freda got together to write the report. By the time they finished, they'd learned a lot about fairness and equality. They were surprised to learn how much work fairness could be.

## Talk About It

Do you think everyone in your school or neighborhood is treated fairly and equally? What can you do to create more equality?

# Give Her a Chance

Abby pushed Beth's wheelchair up to the school bulletin board. "Hurry up!" Beth urged. "Read it to me, read it to me!" It was the first day of school and lots of kids huddled around the class lists posted on the board. They were eager to find out who their new teachers would be.

"Yes!" Abby said. "I have Mr. Stanford." She moved her finger down the list. "Oh no," she shrieked. "Beth, you have Mrs. Yardley. They say she makes kids stay after school almost every day."

"I heard she doesn't even *like* kids," their friend Grace added.

"Poor Beth," someone else said. Beth felt her stomach turn into a knot. That evening she complained to her older brother Bill. She repeated what her friends said, and added, "I have the worst teacher in school!" She felt like crying.

"Give your new teacher a chance," Bill urged. "Gossip about teachers isn't always true. I mean, how can both the things you heard today be true? Why would she keep kids late every day if she doesn't like to be *around* kids?" Beth smiled a little at that. Then Bill told her about one of his teachers with a mean reputation. "Everyone told me he would make you do four hours of homework a night! I felt like you feel right now. But Mr. Day ended up being my favorite teacher."

"Okay," Beth said. "I'll try to relax until I can see for myself what my new teacher is like."

## Talk About It

Have you ever judged another person before you got to know him or her? What happened when you did get to know the person?

# Forgiveness

When you have forgiveness you are willing to forgive people when they do something that hurts or upsets you. (You are also able to forgive yourself.) You are willing to let go of any bad feelings you have toward others. Anger and hatred feel bad, but forgiving helps both you and the other person start feeling better about things. Forgiving does not mean the other person is right and you are wrong. It means that you are choosing to be peaceful and let it go.

# The Bragger

Lupe's friends were gossiping about Ann on the playground. Ann had won their school's art contest, and her drawing was made into bookmarks and given to everyone in the school. Meredith really wanted to win, and Ann bragged about her prize. "Everyone knows I'm a better artist than you," she said.

"Give me a break," said Meredith. "You'd think she invented drawing."

"I know," said Josie. "She carries around her sketching pad all the time, like we have to be reminded that she's THE artist. Big deal."

"What a bragger," said Liz.

Lupe was uncomfortable with the mean words. "It's true Ann bragged," Lupe said. "And I know she was mean to you, Meredith. But she *is* our friend. I don't think we should be talking behind her back like this. I think we should talk to her and let her know she's hurting feelings. Then we should forgive her."

"Yeah, well," Meredith said. And the topic was dropped. But later that day Liz came up to Lupe.

"You were right," Liz said. "We all make mistakes. I wish Meredith would forgive Ann."

## Talk About It

If you were Meredith, would you forgive Ann? Why or why not? Do you think a person has to apologize to be forgiven? Why or why not?

# For Giving

Henry's youth group was talking about anger. The counselor asked people from the group what they would do if someone made fun of them or told a lie about them.

"Tell everybody I know what a jerk that person is," Henry volunteered.

"I would tell that person off," said a girl.

"Would you hold onto your anger for a long time, thinking about what happened over and over?" the counselor asked.

"Maybe," DeShawn muttered.

"I would," said Willie.

"Well, you certainly can do all of these things—and probably will sometimes," said the counselor. "But I wonder if any of these things will make you feel as good as forgiving would."

"Feel good?" asked Henry. "I don't understand. Forgiving is what you do for someone else, not yourself."

"Always remember the second part of the word *forgiving: giving*. It's true that you give to others when you forgive, but sometimes you're giving to yourself, too. You know when you're mad at somebody and you can't get them off of your mind? You just get more and more upset? Well, forgiving stops that. You let go of the anger and *give* yourself calmness and good feelings."

## Talk About It

Do you agree that forgiving can be something you give yourself? Can you think of a time you felt better after forgiving someone? What about a time when you forgave but *didn't* feel better? Why did you do it?

# An Untrue Story

When Quincy walked into the classroom he noticed people looking at him funny. Two kids were whispering to each other and nodding at him. *What in the world is going on?* Quincy wondered, as he slid into his seat.

He found out at lunch time. "Is it true you copied your report from the Internet?" Raven asked him.

"No! That's not true at all!" Quincy said.

"Well, that's what Ahmad is telling everyone." Ahmad was Quincy's best friend. Quincy was really hurt. Why would Ahmad spread such a terrible rumor? He saw Ahmad on the playground and went up to him.

"I never cheat, Ahmad. Why are you telling people I did?"

"Aw, it was just a joke," said Ahmad. "I never thought anybody would believe me—everybody knows you don't cheat."

"Not anymore they don't," said Quincy. "People believed you."

Ahmad saw how angry his friend was. "Oh, man, I'm sorry, Q. I didn't mean to hurt your feelings."

"Well, you did." Quincy walked away angrily.

The next day at school he had calmed down. As he walked into the classroom he saw a note on his desk. "I'm sorry," Ahmad had written. "I won't do it again."

Quincy looked at his friend and nodded. "Okay," he said. "I forgive you."

## Talk About It

Why do you think Quincy forgave Ahmad? Do you think this could improve their friendship? Why or why not?

# Email Etiquette

Amelia was checking her email at the library. One new email was from her friend Alonzo. It said: "MAYBE YOU DIDN'T KNOW THIS BUT IT'S MY TURN TO BE HALL MONITOR. LEAVE ME THE BOOK TOMORROW." No "hello," no "how are you," no "good-bye." Amelia was hurt. Normally Alonzo was really nice. Why was he was being so rude?

That night she called him.

"Alonzo," she said. "Are you upset about something? I'll give you the book tomorrow—but you don't have to be rude."

"What?" Alonzo said. "I wasn't rude. That was just a regular email."

"Maybe you should look at it," Amelia said. So he pulled up the email on his screen. "See how it's all in capital letters?" Amelia said. "In email, those letters are like shouting. Did you mean to shout at me? And you sound so crabby in there—you don't even say hello or anything."

"I really didn't mean to sound that way," Alonzo said. "I was just in a hurry. I'm sorry."

"It's okay," Amelia said. "Email can be weird like that. I'm glad you weren't really being mean."

## Talk About It

What might have happened if Amelia didn't call Alonzo to talk about the email? Have you ever had a similar experience with email? Tell about it.

# The Hang Up

Jessie and Erica were arguing on the phone about something that happened at school. "You are *so* wrong," Jessie said, and suddenly there was a click, then silence. Erica stared at the receiver, not believing her friend had hung up on her.

She thought about it for half an hour. Then she called Jessie back. "I do not appreciate being hung up on, Jessie."

"Well, I'm not sorry," Jessie said.

Erica was so mad at Jessie's behavior that she fidgeted through dinner and hardly ate a thing.

"Are you still upset about Jessie?" her mom asked.

"Yes," Erica said. "Friends are *not* supposed to hang up the phone on each other."

"I agree," said her mom. "But you'll probably feel better if you forgive her and try to quit thinking about it."

"I'm too mad to forgive," Erica said.

"But you can learn to forgive," her mom said. "Try this. Imagine one good thing happening to her—something you know she'd really like."

"Well, she'd like to do better in English," said Erica. "So I see her getting an A paper back from her teacher, and she's grinning from ear to ear."

"And how are *you* feeling right now, Erica?"

"Less angry," Erica said. "Better."

## Talk About It

Is it hard to forgive good friends when they hurt you? Why or why not? Why did Erica's mom think Erica would feel better if she forgave Jessie?

# Generosity

If you are generous you enjoy giving to and sharing with others. You like to help others feel good. You are not selfish.

# Saving the Cats

Cameron cuddled the kitten gently in his lap and squeezed drops of milk onto its tiny pink tongue. Then he carefully lay the black kitten back in the box and picked up the orange one to feed it. His grandmother had taken in three kittens after they'd been abandoned near her house. Cameron was helping care for them.

Nana lived at the end of a dead-end street, and people often dumped kittens in the woods by her house. Each time people discarded the animals, Nana did her best to find them homes. One time she had seven kittens to tend to until they were all adopted. The kids in the neighborhood came by each day to help her feed them, like Cameron was doing today.

Suddenly the doorbell rang, and Nana answered it. When she came back, she had a check in her hand. "Look, Cameron," she said. "The neighbors collected this money to help out with the kitties. This will help with food, cat litter, and medicine."

Cameron stroked the orange cat behind the ears and listened to its happy purr. Then he said, "If you want me to shop for that stuff, I could bring it by tomorrow."

"Thanks, Cameron," Nana said. "That would help."

## Talk About It

How many examples of generosity can you find in this story? Who is being generous, and what are they being generous with?

# Mom's Birthday

Tara and Marvin's mom's birthday was coming up soon. They were talking about the big day and what they could give her. They wanted to get her a gift that was unique—something their mom would really love and could only get from them.

"Let's give our *time* as gifts," Marvin said. "Mom always has a list of chores that need doing. It would make her really happy if we said our present was four hours—two from each of us—doing whatever chores she wanted done."

"But I want it to look like a real gift," said Tara. "Something we can wrap up so it looks exciting. Otherwise, we won't have any presents to give her on her birthday."

Marvin agreed. So they each wrote up slips of paper saying, "My gift is two hours of my time to do chores or errands for you." They drew pictures of themselves doing work: Marvin was vacuuming and Tara was dusting. They colored the slips, put them in small boxes, and wrapped them in bright paper. Then they made bows out of ribbon for the tops of their boxes and hid the packages in their rooms.

## Talk About It

Tara and Marvin are being generous with their time. What else can you be generous with?

# Walking Downtown

Theo and his dad were walking downtown on a winter afternoon. People walked quickly along the sidewalk carrying packages and briefcases. The windows of shops were decorated with snowflakes and brightly wrapped gifts.

As Theo and his dad walked around the corner, a man dressed in a Santa Claus suit stood ringing a bell. Beside him was a red kettle for donations.

"Hold on a second," Theo's dad said as he reached into his pocket. He put two dollars in the kettle. The man thanked him, and Theo's dad wished him a good day. Then Theo and his dad continued walking.

When the man was out of earshot, Theo asked his dad why he gave the man money. "You don't know that guy," Theo said. "Why should you give him your money?"

"His organization gives food and clothes to families that don't have enough," Theo's dad answered.

"But we don't know who those families are," Theo said.

"They need help and we can help them," said his dad. "That's all that matters."

## Talk About It

What does Theo's dad mean, "That's all that matters"? Do you agree with him? Why or why not?

# Holiday Cards

Colorful eggs, sunrises, and jelly beans decorated the greeting cards on the kitchen table. As Lisa's family sat at the table for dinner, Lisa looked at the cards. Her favorite one showed a bunny piñata. Inside the card it said, "Have a great holiday! See you at the picnic next week. Love, the Fazios."

Here was one from Lisa's best friend's family. She'd just seen them today. "Why do people send cards on holidays?" she asked her mom. "It seems kind of silly to get cards from people we see all the time."

"I don't know," said her mom, thinking. "I guess it's one way of being generous—with your affection." She spooned potatoes onto her plate.

"I don't get it," Lisa said. "How is that being generous? Cards are just paper. People throw them away." She took the bowl of potatoes her mom was handing her.

"The card's not the generous part," her dad said. "It's the *idea*. Sending someone a card shows that you're thinking about that person in a warm way. That makes people feel good."

"Kind of like mailing them a compliment?" Lisa said.

"'Mailing them a compliment'—I like that," said her mom.

## Talk About It

Have you ever received a special card or letter? If so, how did it make you feel? Do you agree that sending a card is generous? Why or why not?

# The Action Figures

Ivan made a noise like an explosion as he swooped his action figure through the air and into a wall of blocks.

"Watch out!" called Claudio, diving his figure into a house of cards, flattening it.

"Take that!" Ivan yelled back.

The boys had been playing with Ivan's action figures for over an hour—and the room showed it. The den looked like a battleground, with scattered blocks and toys everywhere. Propped-up couch cushions and pillows made a fort in one corner, and an action-figure jump was built out of magazines and books.

As the boys were cleaning up, Claudio thanked Ivan for inviting him over. "Your guys are really cool, Ivan," he said, holding up one of the action figures. "I can't wait until next weekend to play with them again."

Suddenly, Ivan had a thought. "You want to borrow them until then?" he asked.

Claudio's face lit up. "Sure!" he said. So Ivan went to the kitchen for a bag to put his action figures in.

"Have fun," he said. "And see you Saturday."

"Okay," said Claudio as he walked out the door. "And thanks!"

## Talk About It

Why did Ivan lend his action figures to his friend? How do you think Claudio felt when Ivan said he could borrow the figures? How do you think Ivan felt?

# Gratitude

Gratitude means you are thankful and you show it. You appreciate the good things you have. You appreciate what people do for you and give you, and you let them know it.

# The New Gym Teacher

"Okay class, that's it for today," said the new gym teacher, Mrs. Montoya. "See you tomorrow."

As Jane's classmates walked toward the locker room, Jane stuck her hands in her pockets. She had always been shy. Most of the time she just accepted it about herself. It's just the way she was. But sometimes, like right now, her shyness made her mad, because she wanted to say something to Mrs. Montoya.

Jane used to hate gym. She didn't like sports very much, for one thing. Gym class always used to be boring. But now Jane loved it. Mrs. Montoya made it fun. She had them play different games than before, more interesting ones. And they weren't always so competitive. Plus, Mrs. Montoya was funny. Jane felt it was important to tell her teacher how grateful she was—but she was frozen with shyness.

Just then, Mrs. Montoya walked past. "You were really good with the earth ball today, Jane," she said smiling. "You're becoming quite an athlete."

Jane smiled. And then, just as Mrs. Montoya was walking away, she blurted out what she had been wanting to say. "I think it's because you're such a good teacher," she said. "I never liked gym before, but now I do." Then Jane blushed.

Then she noticed something: Mrs. Montoya blushed, too! "Hey, thank you, Jane," she said. "You just made my day!"

## Talk About It

Why did Jane think it was so important to tell Mrs. Montoya how she felt? Why was it hard for her to express her feelings?

# Lucky Me!

Ezra, Taheed, and Jackson were playing video games in Taheed's bedroom. "You sure have a nice house," Ezra said to Taheed. "And you're lucky to have your own room." Ezra shared a room with his younger brother.

"Go in there," said Taheed, pointing to something on the screen. Ezra moved his character across the screen to where Taheed was pointing. "Get him!" Taheed said. Ezra pushed the button on his game controller.

"My brother and I keep begging Dad to let us buy video games," Ezra said. "But he keeps saying no."

Then Jackson spoke up: "Yeah, but your dad's cool, Ezra. He's really funny and he always jokes around with us."

Taheed nodded. "Yeah, and your brother really looks up to you. I wish I had a little brother."

On screen, Ezra unlocked the final level. As he watched the game tally up his bonus points, he realized his friends were right: he *was* lucky.

## Talk About It

Why did Ezra focus on what *Taheed* had instead of noticing the good things *he* had? What do you have to be grateful for? Why?

# Kicking Off the Year

Today was the first assembly of the new school year, and Darius was excited. As sixth-graders, he and his fellow classmates filed in first and took their seats on the gym bleachers. The third-graders sang songs while everyone was being seated. An entire verse of one song was written about their principal. When she heard it and looked up, surprised, Darius and the other students laughed.

Then came the program. The principal introduced the new members of the school safety patrol. Darius was one of them. He held his patrol flag while someone took a picture.

Next the principal showed slides of all the murals the kids had painted on the walls during the summer. They were bright, colorful, and inspiring. She named the students who worked so hard on the project.

The principal concluded the assembly by telling the kids how great they were and how proud the faculty and staff were to be starting a new school year with such great students.

After the assembly, Darius walked back to class with his friends. He liked hearing all those good things about his school and the people in it.

## Talk About It

Why do you think the principal said all those good things about the students and the school? What are some things you appreciate about your school?

# Someone to Talk With

Something was bothering Ron, and he didn't know who to talk to. One night he was hanging around after his scouting meeting.

"Abe," he said to his troop leader. "Do you have a second?"

"Of course," Abe said. "I'm always here to talk. What's on your mind?"

"My parents are adopting another kid," Ron said. "They seem so excited, and I don't want to spoil it for them. So I've even been pretending I'm happy, too."

"But you're not happy?" Abe asked.

"Well, kind of. I'm excited to have a little brother. But I'm nervous about sharing my parents."

Abe thought for a few seconds. Then he said, "Your parents have a *lot* of love to share. I have learned that when I give love, I seem to have more to give. I'm sure it will be the same with your parents."

"Maybe," Ron said.

"Talk to them about how you feel," Abe said. "They may not have a clue you're upset, especially if you've been pretending to be happy."

"Do you think I can change their minds?"

Abe shook his head. "I don't think so, Ron. But I do think you'll feel better."

"Okay, I'll do it," Ron said. He realized he already felt better, just talking to Abe. "Thanks a lot," he said.

"You're welcome," Abe said.

## Talk About It

Why did Ron thank Abe? What's the most important thing Abe did for Ron?

# The Football Game

"Ten, twenty, thirty, hut!" Grandpa Jim called out. Then Bailey hiked the ball to him. The game had begun. Bailey ran around her uncle, who was covering her. Grandpa Jim passed the ball to 6-year-old Randy, who caught it and ran for a touchdown.

"Score!" Randy yelled.

"Nice play!" said Bailey's mom. The whole family was there, split into two teams.

Soon they called halftime and ate their picnic lunch of sandwiches and apples. After a little rest and some joking around about the game, they went back out and played for another half hour. Back at Grandma and Grandpa's house that night, everyone drank hot chocolate and laughed about the game.

"That was fun," Bailey said as she took a sip from her mug.

Everyone else agreed—all except for Randy, who'd fallen asleep on the floor.

When it was time to go, Grandpa Jim carried an exhausted Bailey to the car. As she snuggled in a blanket in the backseat, Bailey said, "Thanks, Grandpa." Then she yawned and pulled the blanket tight around her.

## Talk About It

What about your family are you grateful for? How can you let your family know you're grateful?

# Helpfulness

Helpfulness means you willingly help others. If you are helpful, you make things easier for other people because you want to—not because you expect a reward. You try to be useful, even when no one has specifically asked you for your assistance.

# Making Lunches

Kwai was at the school lunch table. The kids often try to trade their lunches, or parts of them, with each other. Kwai's lunch that day was a peanut butter and jelly sandwich, some carrot sticks with hummus dip, and an orange. When his friend Larry said Kwai's lunch looked good, Kwai said, "Thanks, I made it."

"My mom always makes my lunch," Douglas said.

"Mine, too," said Larry. "What's up with your mom? Is she mean or something? Why do you have to do all the work?"

Kwai looked at his friends in surprise. "She's not mean," he said. "I like to make my own lunch. Mom works hard. I'm glad to do my share." He dipped a carrot in the creamy hummus. "Plus," he added with a grin, "I like my lunches better."

"I'll trade you a cheese and cracker for a carrot with some of that dip," Larry said.

"Looks like you like my lunch better, too," Kwai said.

## Talk About It

Why does Kwai like making his own lunch? In what ways do you help out at home? Can you think of other ways to be helpful? What are they?

# Middle School

One look at Yolanda's face and her brother knew she was upset. "What's the matter?" Mark asked.

"Middle school is so hard," Yolanda said. "Do you have any idea how impossible it is to remember where you sit in seven different classes? And my books are so heavy that my shoulders ache. And there's not enough time to go to my locker between classes." Yolanda started to cry.

"I *do* know how hard it is," Mark said gently. "I've been in middle school, remember? Maybe I can help you."

Yolanda didn't even seem to hear him. She continued with her list of problems. "Look at my notebook," she said. "It's so big and heavy."

"Hey, I have an idea," Mark said. "I have a bunch of different-colored folders you can have. You can pick ones for each subject instead of using that humongous notebook. Would that help?"

"Maybe," Yolanda said. She'd stopped crying now.

"Well, let's go take a look," Mark said, and he led her to his room. She took the folders she needed. Then she gave her big notebook to their little sister to play with.

The next day, school didn't seem so bad. "Thanks a lot, Mark," she said to him when she got home.

"Those folders really made a difference?" he asked.

"A little," said Yolanda. "But I think the biggest difference was just knowing that you wanted to help. It made me feel good."

## Talk About It

Yolanda said the biggest difference was just knowing that her brother wanted to help. Why do you think that is? How important is it to have people "on your side"?

# The Turtle

Preston settled down on the freshly mown grass at camp, the sun on his face. As he cracked open his new mystery book, he noticed out of the corner of his eye a box turtle moving slowly toward the wall that edged much of the lake.

Caught up in his book, Preston was startled to hear a *ker-plunk*. The turtle had jumped—or fallen—into the water. Preston knew box turtles are land turtles and aren't very good swimmers, so he was surprised to see this one swimming toward the diving pier.

Soon the turtle was scratching against the pier, trying to gain a foothold. It couldn't get out. Preston walked out on the pier, picked up the little creature, and carried it back to dry land.

The turtle stared, unblinking, at Preston for a long time. Then it slowly ambled off toward the woods. Preston watched it go, imagining that it might be going back to its family somewhere. Preston was pleased to know he'd helped the turtle to safety.

## Talk About It

Describe a time you helped a person or animal in need. Why did you do it?

# The Spelling Test

As Tochelle and Pierce walked to school together, Tochelle helped Pierce practice for their spelling test that day.

"Spell *mouth*," Tochelle said.

"M-O-U-T-H," Pierce spelled out.

"Right," said Tochelle. "Now spell *clean*."

"C-L-E-N-E," said Pierce.

"Try again," said Tochelle. "Think about the *e* sound in *bean*."

"Oh, right," Pierce replied. "So that's, C-L-E-A-N."

"Great!" said Tochelle. She drilled him on a few more words and reminded Pierce about spelling rules. She gave him hints on how to remember the hardest words. Soon they were at the classroom door. "I think you're all set," Tochelle said. "You'll do fine on this test."

"Thanks for your help," Pierce said.

"Don't worry," said Tochelle. "You'll have a chance to make it up to me—next week, when the history test comes up. I need plenty of help with that, and you're the history star."

"It's a deal," said Pierce, nodding. Then they went inside to take their test.

## Talk About It

In what ways can you help your friends succeed? Has anyone ever helped you with something that was difficult? Tell about it.

# Fixing Tires

Woody and Scott planned a bike ride to the hobby shop to buy some trading cards. Woody looked forward to it, but Scott was *really* excited. He talked all week about the baseball and football cards he wanted. Finally, Saturday morning rolled around: the day of the trip.

Then Scott called Woody with bad news.

"My bike tire is flat," he said. "I think we'll have to cancel the trip to the hobby shop." He sounded really bummed out.

"Wait a minute," Woody said. "I have a flat tire repair kit—patch, glue—everything we need. I'll bring it over and we'll fix your bike together."

Woody showed Scott how to fix the tire. Scott held the bike as Woody applied the glue. Soon the patch was dry, and they were more excited than ever about starting their adventure.

"I've been saving up for a Brett Favre rookie card!" Scott said, climbing onto his bike.

"Well, let's go see if they have one," Woody said as the boys rode off.

## Talk About It

What could Woody have done *besides* helping fix Scott's tire? Think of things that are helpful and things that are not helpful. Why do you think Woody decided to help him fix it?

# Honesty

When you are honest you are truthful. You tell the truth even when it's hard. And you do not cheat, steal, or lie, even if you think you can get away with it.

# Hairstyles

Wendy and Susan were going to the movies, but first they wanted to do something special with their hair. Susan put her long hair in a bun on top of her head. Around the bun she put a beaded scrunchy. It looked very stylish.

Wendy spiked her hair up all over, layering on the hairspray. She liked the way it looked, even though it felt like she was wearing a big, spikey helmet. Just then her mom walked in. "Yikes!" she said, jumping back. "What a crazy hairdo! You're not going to go out in public like that, are you?" Wendy's mom laughed.

After she left the room, Susan put on a spritz of hairspray. "Doesn't that hurt your feelings when your mom says that?" she asked Wendy. "It would hurt mine."

"Not at all," Wendy answered. "She's just giving her opinion. One other time she didn't like my hairstyle but I wore it that way anyhow because *I* liked it, you know?"

"You don't think she's being mean?" Susan asked.

"She isn't saying it to be mean. Sometimes we tease each other, but it's just for fun. I wouldn't like it if she pretended to like something just because she was afraid of hurting my feelings. I'm glad she respects me enough to say what she really thinks."

## Talk About It

Do you think Wendy's mom is being mean? Why or why not? Can you think of a time when being honest might seem mean or cruel? How do you handle those situations?

# Odd One Out

Steve was invited to a party at Charlie's house. They were going to order pizza and watch scary videos. Steve couldn't wait.

But his mom just asked the dreaded question: "Will Charlie's parents be at home?"

Steve didn't answer right away. He knew they wouldn't be there. Charlie's parents often went out for the evening, leaving Charlie on his own. It sounded so grown up to have a party with no adults around. All the guys were excited about it.

Steve still didn't answer. His mom looked at him questioningly.

"Maybe not," he said finally, looking at the floor. Then he looked up and said, "Actually, for sure not."

His mom began to shake her head.

"But Mom," Steve said. "You know you can trust me not to do anything stupid. All the guys are going. Please don't make me be the odd one out."

"The answer is no," said his mother. "And I'd be very surprised, when other parents realize no adults are present, if very many kids actually show up for this party."

"Oh, man!" Steve said, and ran to his room to lay on his bed.

## Talk About It

Why do you think Steve told his mom the truth? Do you think he would have lied if he thought he could get away with it?

# The Test

Stella bit hard on her pencil, concentrating on the last few questions on her quiz, when she noticed a movement out of the corner of her eye. Teresa was motioning to her. Stella realized Teresa was asking to copy some answers from her paper.

Stella shook her head no, but her friend gave her an angry look. Stella never cheated, but she liked Teresa and wanted to become better friends with her. So the next time Teresa poked her, Stella gave in. Glancing to make sure the teacher wasn't looking, she slid her answer sheet to the corner of her desk.

Just then, the teacher looked up and caught Stella's eye. She came down the aisle and said quietly to Stella and Teresa, "I'll see you both after class."

Stella was furious with Teresa. *I can't believe the trouble she got me into,* she thought.

But the more Stella thought about it, the more she began to feel sick inside. It wasn't just Teresa she was angry at. After all, Teresa didn't *make* Stella cheat. Only Stella could make that decision.

## Talk About It

Besides Teresa, who was Stella angry at? Why? Has something like this ever happened to you? Explain.

# The Sand Sculpture

Julio's mom called him into the bathroom. She was pointing at the broken sand sculpture in the wastebasket. The glass was broken and the water had come out. Colored sand oozed through the cracked glass.

"What happened to this?" she asked. He knew the sculpture was important to her because it had been a gift from her dad.

Julio thought for a minute. Guests had been visiting the house for the past week. The four rowdy cousins had just left this morning. Anything could have happened while all those kids were in the house. Maybe he could blame them.

But Julio knew he could never lie to his mom. "I did it, Mom," he said. "I stepped on it accidentally. I was waiting until everyone left to tell you about it."

His mom got mad at first, but then she calmed down. She told him how much his honesty meant to her. "Thank you for telling me the truth," she said.

That night, Julio found another sculpture on the Internet, and, with his dad's permission, he ordered it to replace the broken one.

## Talk About It

Describe a time it was hard to tell the truth. Why was it hard? How did you handle it?

# Puppies and Friends

Bo lay on the grass in the backyard as the St. Bernard puppies climbed all over her. She stayed outside most of the afternoon until it was time for Mama Dog to feed her pups. Bo smiled as she watched the little ones nuzzle up to their mom.

But when Bo went in the house she got a sinking feeling in her stomach. She had forgotten to go to Kirsten's volleyball game. *She's really going to be upset with me,* Bo thought. Her friend had reminded her about the big game that afternoon at school and then coming home on the bus. Bo knew the game was really important to Kirsten, but when she got around those puppies, she just lost all sense of time.

Bo decided she would tell a little white lie. She could say that she couldn't get a ride. Kirsten would never know. Her feelings wouldn't be hurt, and Bo might not feel so guilty. She dialed Kirsten's number.

When she heard her friend's voice on the phone, Bo realized she couldn't go through with her plan to lie. Instead, she just blurted out the truth. "I was outside playing with the puppies, and I lost track of time. I'm really sorry I forgot about your game," Bo said. "Did you win? How did you play? Can I come next week?"

"We won," Kirsten said. "And I had two excellent spikes. I wish you had been there."

"I'm sorry," Bo said. "I wish I had been there, too."

## Talk About It

How did Bo show integrity? How would this story have ended if Bo had told Kirsten the lie instead of the truth? How would Bo have felt? Have you ever told a lie to keep yourself out of trouble? What happened?

# Integrity

Having integrity means trying to be honest and true to your beliefs at *all* times, no matter where you are or what's going on. Having integrity doesn't mean you never change your mind; it means you don't change your beliefs or values for different situations. People know what they can expect from you; you won't change to fit in or be popular.

# The New Girl in School

Sylvia transferred into Ashley's school last week. She was very tall, and Ashley's friends teased her, calling her "Stork" and other mean names. Sylvia sat alone in the lunch room, she sat by herself in the library, and the other girls even talked about her behind her back.

Ashley felt sorry for Sylvia. "I don't think we're being fair to her," she told her friends one day at recess. "She might be real nice. I vote we help her out a bit."

"Oh, yeah, like you helped out Donnie Barber when he started at this school," said Kaitlin. "You made fun of him more than anyone else did."

"Well, that's different," Ashley said. "He's a boy."

"It's not different at all," Kaitlin said. "He's a person. He wants people to like him, just like everyone else."

Ashley realized Kaitlin was right. She had been using different standards for how to treat people, and she didn't even know it. She had been mean to Donnie. Just like her friends were being to Sylvia.

## Talk About It

What can Ashley do to make up for being mean to Donnie—and show more integrity?

# Electing to Be Me

The fifth grade at Reggie's school was electing a class president. Reggie decided to run. One day, he and the other candidate gave speeches to the class. It was a chance to tell the other kids about their ideas and what they would do if elected.

Reggie stood in front of the students and spoke clearly and loudly. When he said, "We need to have a study period," some kids cheered and waved flags. But other kids booed. Reggie was a little confused, but he went on. "If elected, I will ask the school to sell fruit," he said. "Students deserve snacks that aren't junk food from vending machines." Once again, some students cheered while others booed and yelled.

After the speeches, Reggie talked to his friend Buzz. "How am I going to make everybody happy?" he asked. "I want everyone to vote for me. But how will they, when one person wants one thing and another wants something totally different?"

"Man, I don't know," Buzz said. "I don't think you can please everybody. If you try, you'll be like a dog chasing its tail—you'll never get anywhere, just dizzy."

"I guess the only way not to offend anyone is just to keep my mouth shut," Reggie said.

"And then you'd bother someone else for being a wimp!" said Buzz, and the boys laughed.

## Talk About It

What do you think Reggie should do? Why? What are some other situations when you might feel pressure—like Reggie did—to try to please different people who want different things? How can you handle those situations?

# Always a Friend

Marcello and Freddy had a great weekend playing together. The neighbors built a fort in the woods. They played softball at the park. And Saturday night, Marcello's parents invited Freddy over for dinner.

But something happened at school on Monday. Some popular kids started teasing Freddy—and Marcello was with them! One kid flipped Freddy's cap off his head, and when Freddy bent down to pick it up another kid pushed him over. Everyone laughed, even Marcello. Freddy sat on the ground and put his cap on. "What a nerd," one kid said.

"Hey, baby, are you going to cry?" said another.

"Yeah," Marcello added. "Don't cry now, baby!"

Freddy felt like he *might* cry. He thought Marcello was his friend. What was going on? That night he called him. "Why did you pick on me today?" he asked.

"I don't know," Marcello said. "I guess I really want those kids to like me. They're so cool."

"I don't think they're cool," Freddy said. "Being a friend means you're respectful, and not just when it's easy."

## Talk About It

Do you think Marcello is really Freddy's friend? If so, what can he do to show Freddy he is?

# The Old House

Anowar and his brothers were exploring the wooded area behind their apartment building when they found an old shack. The windows were broken, the paint was cracked and peeling, and the porch had boards missing. Obviously, the house had been abandoned a long time ago. It looked like something out of a scary movie. Everyone wanted to check it out.

The door creaked as they forced it open. "Ugh," said Anowar as he pulled a sticky cobweb from his face.

The old house wasn't so exciting once they got in. Just lots of dust and papers. But then Anowar's brothers noticed a wooden rocking chair in the corner. It looked like an antique, something their mother would like. And it was in good shape.

"Let's take it home and polish it up for Mom for Mother's Day," said Joe. Their younger brother nodded. "The three of us could get it home. I bet Mrs. Jenkins would store it for us until Mother's Day."

"Wait a minute," said Anowar. "Even if this house is abandoned, the chair doesn't belong to us. I don't think we should take it."

"But someone left it here," said Joe. "Nobody's going to miss it."

"You wouldn't steal a chair out of someone's house or a store," said Anowar. "Why would you take this? Somebody owns this land and this house—and this chair."

## Talk About It

Do you agree with Anowar? Why or why not? What does this story have to do with integrity?

# The Sleepover

Elaine's new friend Angelica was very popular at school. She was funny, for one thing. She could make you crack up laughing during class. Everyone liked to work with her on homework and projects because she made work seem fun. And she was nice to her schoolmates and teachers.

On Friday night Elaine went to Angelica's for a sleepover. When she carried her sleeping bag and backpack in the front door, she saw Angelica's mom sitting on the couch. Her mom smiled, but Angelica said, "Come on," and led Elaine to her room without introducing her mom. At dinner, Angelica's mom asked the girls if they'd like some corn, and Angelica said, "No, Mom, we don't want any gross corn. I think you *know* I don't like corn." After dinner Angelica didn't help her mom clean up the dishes.

That night, as they lay in bed in the dark, Angelica told a couple of her famous jokes. But Elaine only pretended to laugh. She was thinking. She had always thought Angelica was so nice, but she sure didn't treat her mom very well. Elaine wasn't sure what Angelica was really like anymore.

## Talk About It

Why did the way Angelica treated her mom bother Elaine so much? Do you treat your family and friends the same?

# Kindness

Kindness means enjoying doing positive things for others. A kind person wants to make other people happy. You can show kindness by being gentle, helpful, and friendly. You ask for nothing in return, but if you're kind, most people will be kind to you, too.

# Two Pitchers

Stan and his teammate Dustin were playing catch when Stan told his big news. "Coach is going to let me pitch a game next week," he said.

The throw from Dustin landed in Stan's glove with a snap. Dustin had a great arm. Stan took the ball out of his glove and held it in his hand. He rubbed the seams and practiced holding it the way his coach showed him a pitcher should. He waited to see what Dustin would say. Dustin was already a pitcher on the team, and a good one. Would he be mad that Stan was going to pitch, too? That might mean less pitching time for him.

"That's great, Stan," his friend said. "You've worked hard and you deserve it."

"Thanks," Stan said. "I'm really excited—and nervous. Everyone will be watching me. What if I walk a lot of batters?"

"It *can* make you nervous," Dustin said. "But that's part of what makes it fun. Want me to teach you my fastball?"

Stan nodded as Dustin jogged toward him. He was glad his friend was happy for him. And he'd take any help he could get.

## Talk About It

Why did Stan think Dustin might be mad? How do you think Dustin did feel? Is it sometimes hard to feel happy for another's success? Why?

# Dad and the Fat Cat

Elsa looked out her bedroom window. There, at the far end of the backyard, was her dad, sitting in the big outdoor chair. Elsa was startled to see her fat gray cat, Smoky, sitting with him, curled up in his lap. Bright sun shined on them as they dozed in the warm spring air. They both looked perfectly content.

Elsa was surprised because two weeks ago, before they'd gotten the cat, Dad had argued against it. "They're stinky," he said. "I don't want a litter box stinking up the house. And food and litter are expensive. Besides, I'm just not a cat person." Elsa had begged him to change his mind, and finally he did. But in two weeks Dad hadn't paid any attention to Smoky. He wasn't mean to the cat—he just didn't notice it.

Elsa brought a glass of water down to her dad. "So, I thought you didn't like cats, huh, Dad?" she said, teasing him. "Maybe you're a cat person after all."

"Hey," Dad said, rubbing Smoky behind the ears. "Just because I don't like cats doesn't mean I can't be nice to them."

## Talk About It

Why was Elsa's dad nice to Smoky if he didn't like cats?

# Friends and Little Brothers

Mort and Tyson were playing checkers on the concrete table at the city park. Mort's little brother was along. For a while he was swinging and sliding and having a great time, but eventually he was hanging out with the bigger boys. "I want to play checkers, too," he said.

"You can't play checkers with three people, Jimbo," Mort said. "Now go and play."

Tyson moved one of his pieces onto Mort's back row. "King me," he said to Mort.

"I don't want to play by myself anymore," Jimbo said, as his big brother put a black checker on top of Tyson's piece. "I'd rather play with you guys."

"I'll tell you what," Tyson piped up. "Why don't you sit with me and help me make some moves? Do you mind, Mort?" Mort just shrugged, so Jimbo crawled next to Tyson on the bench.

"Now here," Tyson said to Jimbo after Mort had made his move. "Look at this. I can move this guy here, or I can move that one to there. Which do you think?"

"That one," Jimbo said.

"Yeah, I think you're right," said Tyson.

## Talk About It

How do you think Jimbo felt when Tyson let him play? How do you think Tyson felt? What are some ways children can show kindness to their brothers and sisters?

# Shoot Some Hoops

Virginia jumped up and tossed the basketball toward the basket, but it hit the rim and bounced away. "You never make jump shots," her sister Carlie said. "Why do you keep trying?"

"I'm doing the best I can," Virginia muttered.

"Now you've missed a pass!" Carlie yelled as the ball whizzed past her sister. Her harsh words were punctuated by the ball bouncing on the hard concrete. "We could just end the game right now if you're not even going to try."

"I am trying!" Virginia said.

"I'm out of here," Carlie shouted, and stomped off in the disgust. "Maybe you should try kickball, little sister."

Virginia dribbled the ball up and down the driveway and practiced making baskets. Soon she heard bicycle tires stopping behind her.

"Let's shoot some hoops!" her best friend Olivia called out. As the girls dribbled and shot, other neighborhood kids joined in. They played until it was almost too dark to see. There was time for one more play. The score was tied and Virginia had the ball.

"Put it in, Virginia!" Olivia cheered. "Make the shot. You can do it."

Virginia held the ball on the fingertips of one hand and jumped up, lofting the ball toward the basket. Then she and her friends watched as it came down, down, and—*boing!*—bounced off the rim.

"Nice try!" Olivia yelled.

## Talk About It

What is the difference between the ways Carlie and Olivia treated Virginia? Be specific. Do you think Virginia should play with Carlie any more? Why or why not?

# Milk Run

Molly and Powell were walking home from school together. "Are we meeting to start our Earth Day homework?" Molly asked. This was their usual routine. Their houses were next door to each other and their parents were friends. The kids often went to each other's place after school to have a snack, work on homework, and maybe watch a little TV.

"I don't know if I can fit it in today," said Powell. "Mom asked me to pick up milk at the store. Then I'm supposed to vacuum. She's got some meeting tonight at the house."

"Do you want me to pick up the milk for you?" Molly offered. "Then you could get a head start on the vacuuming. Maybe we'd still have time to talk about the Earth Day project." She held up the book she'd found at the library. "I think I've got a good source here."

"I probably still wouldn't have time," Powell said. "I've also got to do the dishes and clean my room. She really wants the place to look good tonight."

"Well, I could still get the milk for you if it would help."

"Yeah, okay," Powell said. "It would be a huge help."

As they reached Powell's door, he handed Molly the milk money. Then he ran inside to get the vacuuming done.

## Talk About It

Molly helped Powell even though he wouldn't be able to come over later. How do you think that made Powell feel? How do you think it made Molly feel? Talk about a time when you did something kind for someone.

# Leadership

A leader sets a positive example for others. Leaders behave in ways that make others look up to them or want to follow them. Leadership means doing new things first, so others can see how they're done and can follow. It also means doing what needs to be done to get through a hard time or crisis.

# City Gardening

When Chip's dad got a new job, his family moved to an apartment in the city. The building was small but had lots of kids living there. Chip made friends easily and enjoyed living so close to his new buddies. So he wasn't too homesick for the country.

But when spring came, Chip knew he was going to miss planting a garden. He loved working in the dirt and watching the plants come up. Eating home-grown watermelon and having seed-spitting contests were great fun. And his favorite summer sandwich was a BLT made with lettuce and tomatoes from his own garden. He decided to try and persuade his friends into helping him grow a small garden.

"Where would we do that? This is the city—not a farm," Roy teased.

"Yeah, I don't even like vegetables, so I sure wouldn't want to grow them," Benjie added.

"Listen," Chip said. "We can use the area behind the building. Dad and I talked to the building super yesterday. He likes the idea as long as we share our tomatoes with him. We'd need to decide how much we can plant. It will have to be figured out mathematically."

Roy really liked math so that part got his attention. "I can figure that out," he said. "But I don't know about digging in the dirt. That dirt's as hard as a brick." And although Benjie didn't like vegetables, he did like watermelon, so when Chip said they could grow a couple watermelon plants, he agreed to help, too.

The next Saturday Chip's dad rented a tiller and helped the boys loosen up the dirt. Roy made a planting plan of mathematical precision. He figured out exactly how much space each plant would take. He found out he could get more things to grow by using stakes and heavy string. It amazed the others how much could be grown in the small area. And after the soil was tilled, Roy decided he wanted to help plant, too.

The boys kept the garden watered, fertilized, and weeded. In the summer they had tomatoes, some pole beans, and several watermelons. When the watermelons were ripe, they invited other kids to share. And they had awesome seed-spitting contests.

"We'll probably have watermelons cropping up all over next summer," Chip said as watermelon seeds flew.

## Talk About It

Why didn't Chip just make the garden by himself? Why did Benjie and Roy finally agree to help with it? In what ways did Chip show leadership?

# Keeping in Line

"Why can't I be the line leader?" Cassie whined.

"You'll never be picked to be line leader," Ethan said. "You don't stay in line well yourself, and sometimes you poke other kids."

What Ethan said hurt Cassie's feelings, but she knew it was true. She was a wiggle worm and sometimes she talked when her third-grade class was supposed to be quiet walking down the hall.

Still, she thought it would be great to have the whole class follow her all the way to the cafeteria. So Cassie made a decision. If she was going to be the leader, she had to be on her best behavior in line to show that she deserved it.

At first it was hard. When other kids giggled, she was tempted to join in. Once she had a great joke she wanted to share, but she kept it to herself. Whenever she felt like wandering or spinning or dancing or hopping out of line, she reminded herself to stay calm. And when it seemed like the perfect moment to poke someone, she kept her arms at her sides.

Soon the day came. "Cassie, would you like to lead us down to the lunch room?" her teacher asked one morning.

"Yes!" Cassie said, and went to the door as the line formed behind her. Again, as they walked to the lunch room, she was on her best behavior.

## Talk About It

Why did Cassie want to be the line leader? Why did she have to prove she could behave in line before the teacher would let her be the leader? Do you think good leaders are also good followers? Why or why not?

# The Book Club

The fifth-grade class at Leah's elementary school raised enough money to buy 25 new books for the school library. The students looked through catalogs and voted on which books to order. Leah and her friends were excited about the new books.

"Wouldn't it be great to form a book club?" Leah said to her friends. "We could read a new book every month and meet to discuss it." The other kids liked the idea, but they thought it would be a lot of work.

"Where would we meet?" Tiara asked. "How would we decide which books to read?"

"Yeah, it sounds like fun, but I don't think it will happen," said Bobby.

"I'll figure it out," Leah said.

Leah asked her homeroom teacher, Mr. Burns, if he would be the group's teacher sponsor. He was happy to do it. Mr. Burns said they needed to get permission from the principal to have the club. "He will also have to approve the time and place that we meet," he said. So Leah, Tiara, and Bobby went to see the principal that week. The principal thought it was a great idea and suggested they meet in the library. The kids then met with the librarian, and it was all set.

"We have a time, a place, a teacher sponsor, and we can vote on which books to read," Leah said. "At our first meeting, we can make posters inviting other kids to join."

"That sounds excellent," said Bobby.

## Talk About It

What did Leah do to show she was a good leader? Do you think the book club would have happened without Leah's persistence? Why or why not?

# Hurricane Help

Stories of the hurricane that hit the Gulf Coast were on the news for days. Angel couldn't believe all the harm that was caused. She and her friends talked about it a lot. Angel wanted to do something to help, but she wasn't sure what to do.

That Sunday morning, she learned her church had opened its campground to several families displaced by the hurricane. There were eight children living with their parents there.

Angel finally knew what to do. She decided to collect donations to make a packet for each kid. The kids needed lots of things.

Angel called her friends. They agreed to meet that afternoon. She went over her ideas with them and asked for their ideas. "My uncle's a dentist," Harold said. "I bet he'll donate toothbrushes and toothpaste."

"We can get crayons and coloring books for a dollar each at the discount store," Camilla said. "I know our friends will donate a dollar a piece to buy them."

"What about toys?" Tracie asked. "Kids need toys."

"You're right, but that may get expensive," Angel replied. She thought for a moment and said, "I have a brand-new stuffed animal I haven't even touched yet. I'll ask my mom if I can donate that. Maybe we can collect other new, or almost-new, toys from kids at school."

"Sure—I can give," said Harold. The others nodded in agreement. In two days they had packets for every child at the camp.

## Talk About It

What might have happened if Angel hadn't called her friends to help collect the donations?

# Wrappers and Cans

Taylor loved to go to the recreation center at his apartment complex. The outdoor basketball court was his favorite place to meet his friends. Inside were lots of board games to play. So rain or shine, he and his buddies had a place to go.

One afternoon as Taylor was walking up the sidewalk to the center, he noticed a few candy and gum wrappers close to the entryway. His friends were sitting on the curb waiting for him. Taylor picked up the trash and put it in the garbage can beside the door. Then they all went to play basketball.

Taylor and his buddies played hard, and they were wiped out afterward. "I could use a snack to charge up," Taylor said. So the boys went inside the center to get a soda and some pretzels.

Sitting outside and snacking, the boys talked about the game. Then, as they were getting up to leave, Greg wadded up his candy wrapper and let it drop to the ground. Nigel tried to toss his soda can into the recycling bin and missed.

"Oh well, no points for that one," Nigel said, walking away. Taylor didn't say anything, but he picked up the litter and put it where it belonged.

## Talk About It

Do you think Taylor should have said something to his friends about their littering? Why do you think he didn't? Did he still show leadership? If so, how?

# Loyalty

Loyalty is being faithful to a belief, person, or group. When you are loyal, others know you won't abandon them if things are tough. They can depend on you.

# Sticking Up for a Buddy

Some kids were giving Nolan a hard time in gym class. "Hey blimpy, nice legs!" someone said.

"Don't put the fatso on my team," said someone else.

Nolan grinned weakly and acted like it was no big deal, but Anna knew better. Nolan had been her friend since kindergarten, and she knew this teasing hurt him. She wanted to speak up, but it was hard. All the kids were laughing—if she stuck up for Nolan they might make fun of her, too.

"Let's make Nolan the goalie," someone said. "Nothing could get past that huge gut."

Finally, Anna couldn't stand it any more. "Knock it off, you guys!" she said. "How would you feel if people treated you that way?"

One of the kids said, "He doesn't care. Look at him." Nolan stood there, still trying to smile.

"Well," said Anna, "if you don't want to stop for his feelings, then stop for mine. He's my friend, and it hurts me to hear you say these things."

## Talk About It

Have you ever had trouble sticking up for a friend? Why was it hard? Has anyone ever stuck up for you? If so, how did it make you feel?

# At the Festival

Joel and Dennis were at a street festival, waiting in line to buy fresh-squeezed lemonade. The smell of funnel cakes filled the air, along with the sounds of a rock band playing on the next block.

"Could you believe Phil in school yesterday?" Dennis said. "He must have raised his hand with the right answer five times. I can't stand kids who show off like that."

"Maybe he just knew the answers," Joel said. "Give him a break." Joel didn't like to hear kids talking behind each other's backs.

"Oh, I forgot," said Dennis. "You're another one of those know-it-alls."

"I am not," Joel said.

"Sure you are. Just ask any of the guys. We were all laughing about it yesterday, what a big know-it-all you are."

"You were making fun of me?" Joel asked. He was really hurt, though he wasn't surprised. Dennis had made fun of him before. Dennis made fun of lots of people.

That night, Joel's mom asked him if he wanted to invite Dennis over for dinner.

"No thanks, Mom," Joel told her. "Dennis makes fun of me and other kids a lot. I'm not going to hang out with him for a while. Until he learns to be more loyal to his friends."

## Talk About It

Is teasing the same as making fun? If not, what's the difference? Do you think Joel is being loyal to Dennis? Why or why not? What could Joel do instead of stopping hanging out with Dennis?

# Team Spirit

Hua's soccer team used to be in first place. But they'd lost a few games in a row recently, and now they were in third. "It's no wonder," Hua said grumpily to herself. "Janell has been more interested in boys lately than soccer, and it's showing." And their goalie, Eleanor, had been giving up a lot of goals. She wasn't concentrating hard enough. In fact, the more Hua thought about it, her whole team seemed to be slacking off. They were just no good anymore. Hua thought maybe she ought to just quit.

At practice that night, Eleanor called a team meeting.

"I've heard some people saying we used to be a great team," Eleanor said. "Well, I think we're *still* a great team. We've played some good teams lately, and we need to sharpen some of our skills."

"You're right," said Janell. "You don't get to be third place if you're not good. And I think we can do better."

Hua watched her teammates' shoulders stand up a little taller. Smiles were on their faces as they raised their fists in the air. Hua joined them, putting her arms around a couple of teammates. *Being part of a team is great,* she thought, *good times and bad.*

## Talk About It

Why is it easier to be loyal to a team or friends or something else when things are going well? Why is it important to be loyal even when things are going badly?

# The Rec Center

Diego's friends were planning to see a movie late Friday night. Harley's dad was taking them. It was the opening night, and everyone was excited. But Thursday after school, when Diego asked his parents if he could join the guys, his dad reminded him they had plans for Saturday morning. His dad coached a basketball team of six- and seven-year-olds at the rec center. Diego had promised to help him run some drills Saturday. "I think you better skip the movie," his dad said. "We have to be at the gym pretty early, and I don't want you to be tired."

Friday morning at school, Diego told his friends he couldn't go with them. "Man, that stinks," Harley said.

"I know," Diego agreed. Usually he really liked working with the younger boys, but right now he was just mad. He'd rather go out with his friends.

That afternoon, Trent came up to him at the bike racks. "Hey, can I come with you to the rec center?" Trent asked. "I think that sounds fun."

"Okay," Diego said, unlocking his bike. "It *is* fun. I think you'll like the kids."

## Talk About It

How many examples of loyalty can you find in this story? Can you think of a time when it was hard to be loyal to people who depended on you?

# Crosswords and Coffee

"This one's easy," Vincent said to his grandfather. "A three-letter word for an insect. It has to be *bug*." He took his pencil and carefully wrote *bug* as the answer to number three down on the crossword puzzle. He could usually figure out the small words, but it took his grandfather to get the big ones.

Working the crossword puzzle with his grandfather was a Saturday morning ritual. Papa was 83 years old and could not see well enough to do the puzzles by himself any more. But his mind was sharp, and his favorite thing was to do crossword puzzles, especially with his grandson.

Vincent and Papa sipped their coffee as they thought about the words. Actually, Vincent's drink was mostly milk with only a little coffee in his cup, but he felt like a grown-up drinking coffee with Papa.

"Did you figure out what the eleven-letter word for *impounded* is?" Vincent asked. "It ends with *cated* and we now have the first two letters: *c* and *o*."

Papa grinned really big. "It's *confiscated!*" he said. He spelled the word as Vincent wrote it down. Sure enough, it fit. He always got excited whenever they figured out a big word.

Vincent loved his Saturday mornings with Papa. Even though sometimes—like today—his friends wanted him to play, he never skipped his Saturday ritual. After all, he could play with his friends all afternoon if he wanted to.

## Talk About It

Why does it sometimes sound more fun to do things with friends instead of with family? Why is being loyal to both groups important? How can you be loyal to both groups?

# Patience

When you have patience you are willing to wait for what you want, need, or deserve—without complaining or giving up. This requires self-control. It means you do not act recklessly, without thinking.

# Homecoming

C armen took the calendar off the refrigerator door and put a big red X on today's date. Only 10 more days until her mom would be home. Her mom was a sergeant in the army and had been overseas for 12 months. It seemed like forever.

"Aunt Judy," Carmen called out. "Ten more days! I don't know how we can wait that long. I feel like jumping out of my skin."

"I'll be there in a minute," Aunt Judy said. "I'm feeding Joseph."

Carmen missed her mom so much. She had a lot to tell her about what she'd been up to. She knew her mom also would have plenty of stories and pictures to share. She also might have souvenirs from the country she'd been in.

But the absolute most special thing would be when Mom meets her sister's new son, Joseph, for the first time. Carmen's little cousin was born two months after her mom left, so she had never seen him.

Aunt Judy carried the baby into the kitchen. "It's so hard to have patience at a time like this," she said. "I miss my sis." She bounced the baby on her lap as the two sat and drank a cup of tea.

"Let's plan some of the things we'll do when Mom comes home," Carmen said. "That will help pass the time away."

## Talk About It

What else can Carmen and her aunt do to help them be patient?

# Computer Helper

Ibrahim's family got a new computer and it was driving everyone nuts. Everybody but Ibrahim, that is. Unlike his parents, Ibrahim understood computers. He loved working with new software and figuring out what to do when he ran into problems.

His dad asked for a lot of help from Ibrahim over the first few weeks they had the machine. Ibrahim took his time explaining things. He showed his dad that the computer had a program to tutor him. "And you can put everyone's email address in this address book," he said to his dad. "Then, you just type in the person's name when you want to email them." It was all very simple to him, but his dad struggled.

"I don't get it," his dad said, time and time again. Ibrahim was frustrated, especially because he couldn't spend as much time on the computer as he wanted while his dad was learning. But finally it began to sink in. "You'll never believe this," his dad said one night. "But I think your patience has finally paid off. I just sent an email without any help."

That night Ibrahim downloaded a beautiful screensaver with a picture of bike riders at the Tour de France. The sun streamed down on the colorful bikes and their even more colorful outfits. It would be a surprise for his dad next time he logged on. Both Ibrahim and his dad loved to ride bikes. He couldn't wait for his dad to discover it.

## Talk About It

Have you ever taught someone a new skill? Was it hard to be patient? Why or why not?

# Dancing Steps

Allie was glad it was September because dance class started again. Practicing every day and spending two hours in class each week didn't bother her at all. She loved to dance.

One night before her class, Allie was talking with her friend Beverly.

"I'm so excited," she said. "We get to start learning our recital numbers tonight." She'd been looking forward to the winter recital ever since her spring recital ended.

"Isn't this a little early?" Beverly asked. "Your recital isn't until December. I think I'd get impatient waiting three months for one important night."

"Getting ready for the recital is just as much fun as the recital itself," Allie said. "I like every part of it: learning the steps and dances, practicing them, getting our costumes . . . practicing some more!"

"It's still a long time to work on one thing," Beverly said.

"It is hard to wait sometimes, but then I just think about how much fun I'm having. Actually, the waiting and the build-up are the best part."

"Better than the big night itself?" Beverly asked.

"Well . . . maybe," Allie said, laughing.

## Talk About It

What does Allie do to help herself be patient? Why do you think Beverly thinks the wait will be so hard?

# What I Want to Be

Marieka was staring off into space, chewing on her fingernails, when her dad came into the room.

"What's up, kiddo?" he asked. "You're going to chew your fingers off!"

"I can't decide what I want to be when I grow up," Marieka sighed. "I want to be a pilot or an architect. But I also want to be a painter, too. They'd all be excellent."

"You're right, those are some pretty excellent options," her dad said.

"That's why it's so hard to choose," Marieka said.

"Why choose?" her dad asked. "Your mom is a chemist, but she also volunteers in your school library sometimes. She's also an athlete—and she paints, too."

"But what if I can never decide?" Marieka asked. "I mean, if I want to be a pilot, I need to start raising my math grades right *now*."

Her father laughed. "You don't need to worry quite so much just yet. When the time is closer for you to have a career, you can explore your options then. Right now, you have time to enjoy being a kid."

## Talk About It

Why is it sometimes hard to be patient about growing up? What are some good reasons to *be* patient?

# The Music Player

Sahid wanted a hand-held digital music player so bad he could taste it. He looked at them in store windows. He saw the ads on TV. He even knew what color he wanted: electric blue.

Sahid certainly couldn't afford the music player by himself, so he pleaded with his mom to buy it for him. Sahid already did a lot of extra chores around the house, so neither he nor his mom thought adding on more chores to help pay for the player was a good idea.

"Sounds like you need to wait for your birthday," said Sahid's mom. "And you need to know it will be your only gift because it's a big one."

"But my birthday is five months away," said Sahid. That meant going through the rest of the school year without the player.

But Sahid accepted his mom's suggestion. He tried not to think so much about the music player. And when he thought about walking to school with his earphones on, he just kept telling himself his gift would be worth the wait.

## Talk About It

Describe a time when you had to wait for something you really wanted. Was it hard to stay patient? Why?

# Peacefulness

Peacefulness means working to avoid violence and resolve conflicts. If you are a peaceful person you value peace. When conflicts arise between people, you try to solve them in ways that hurt no one.

# Using Their Brains

Nelson and Dakota were brothers and best buddies. They both earned high grades at school, and they knew computers inside and out. On their way home from school one day some kids in the neighborhood started teasing them and calling them names.

"Hey, nerds!" one kid called out.

"Hey, computer geeks, come over here and do my homework," another yelled.

"Yeah, I'll come over there," Nelson said to Dakota. He was a couple years older than his brother, and he was bigger than the bullies. "I'll show them to leave us alone."

"No," Dakota said. "Let's not get in a fight."

Nelson agreed, but the teasing went on the rest of the week. Dakota and Nelson were getting tired of it. "I'd like to beat up those jerks," Nelson said.

"Instead of fighting, let's put our brains to use and come up with a peaceful solution," Dakota said.

The boys decided to walk a different route home, so they wouldn't run into the other kids any more. At first Nelson was mad that he had to change his route just because of those other kids, but soon he began to like the new way. They passed by a little store every day, and he could buy a snack if he wanted to. And he was glad he didn't get into trouble for fighting.

## Talk About It

Do you think going a different way was the best solution for Nelson and Dakota? Why or why not? What else could they have done?

# The Agreement

Hannah had been in class with her good friend Kris every year since kindergarten, and sixth grade was no different: they both had Mr. Keith. But this year, Hannah's other friend, Jo, was in their class, too.

Kris and Jo didn't get along too well. They each tried to be Hannah's best friend, and they each talked behind the other's back. "Kris's top is *so* ugly," Jo said to Hannah one day. "Jo thinks she's so good at softball, but everyone knows she stinks," said Kris another time. As the year wore on, Kris and Jo fought and fought. Hannah was always in the middle.

"This fighting has to stop," she said one day. "Come to my house tomorrow, and we'll figure out a way to end the fighting."

That next morning was Saturday. Hannah wrote "Peace Agreement" at the top of a sheet of paper. She asked her friends to agree to the following terms: take turns playing with Hannah at recess, stop making nasty remarks to each other, refrain from exchanging mean looks, and never complain about the other one to Hannah.

All three girls signed the agreement.

Secretly, both Kris and Jo thought the other one would never keep the agreement. They both wanted to stay friends with Hannah, though, so they were willing to try. To their amazement, the weeks ticked by without many fights. They'd start, but then remember the agreement. Sometimes, the girls even enjoyed playing together.

## Talk About It

Describe a time you found yourself stuck between two friends who were fighting. How did it feel? What did you do?

# Mental Muscles

Chad and his neighbor Arthur were riding to school with Chad's mom. The boys were in the backseat, bragging to each other about how strong their dads were. Arthur said, "My dad is way stronger than your dad."

"No way," Chad said. "My dad could *totally* beat up your dad."

After school that night, Chad's mom talked to him. "Chad, have you ever seen your dad hit someone?"

"No," said Chad.

"If you saw him get so angry he hit someone, would you think he was stronger because he did?" his mom asked. Chad squirmed, but didn't say anything. "Okay," she went on. "Let's say two fathers catch their sons telling lies. One father hits his son. The other dad is also very mad, but he sits down and talks with his son. Which dad is stronger?"

"Mom, I was talking about muscles," Chad said. "Using your muscles means you're stronger. I'd like the second dad better, but that wouldn't mean he's stronger."

"Are you sure?" his mom asked. "It takes strength to stay calm and not throw your weight around."

"Sort of like mental muscles?" Chad asked.

"Yeah," said his mom.

## Talk About It

What are some ways you can show strength without using your muscles? Tell about a time you've done so.

# Neighborhood Chores

Eduardo's friend Johnny had worked in their neighborhood for two summers. He did chores for people and got paid to do them. Eduardo's other friend Sim was new in the neighborhood. He loved doing summer work and getting paid, too. Johnny didn't want to lose any business and thought all the neighbors should use him and not use Sim.

"I saw Sim moving broken tree limbs for Mr. Piron," Johnny complained to Eduardo. "I worked for him last summer. Sim's taking my business."

Later that day Sim came over to Eduardo's home. "Dude, Johnny's giving me a hard time about doing work in the neighborhood," Sim said. "I need to make some money, too. That guy needs to calm down, don't you think?" But Eduardo didn't want to take sides. This was not his argument. He told both of his friends they needed to work it out between themselves.

At first the guys didn't like that. They kept trying to get Eduardo to take their side, and when he wouldn't, they got mad at him. That was rough for a while. But they remained friends and by the end of the summer the boys had worked it out.

## Talk About It

Should Eduardo have done more to make peace between his friends? Why or why not?

# The Peace Vigil

Rachael put on her coat and checked to see if she had the candles in her pocket. She grabbed a blanket and called to her mom to be sure to bring the flashlight.

"Hurry, Mom," she called out. "Let's get there on time."

Rachael had been reading about a civil war in another country for many weeks. The fighting just seemed to get worse and worse. Her rabbi invited all who were interested to gather in front of the temple for a peace vigil. Their demonstration would show they were against the war and hoped for peace. The rabbi encouraged the congregation to invite any interested friends, and Rachael was glad to know that two of her buddies from school would be there with their families, too.

When Rachael arrived, she joined the group of people gathered on the steps of the temple. She lit her candle from the flame of her friend's, and her mom lit hers from Rachael's. They stood side-by-side with the others and sang songs about peace. Rachael thought about all the people who had been hurt or killed. It was heartbreaking to think of all the families broken apart by the war.

As the night grew later, the group grew larger. People of all ages joined in. Children sat on blankets. Adults stood holding their candles. The light of Rachael's candle showed the sad but proud expression on her face.

## Talk About It

Why did these people hold a peace vigil? Do you think holding a peace vigil can make a difference? If so, how?

# Perseverance

Perseverance means not giving up easily. If you want something to happen, you will keep working on it even if it's difficult. You keep trying—even if you have problems or fail at first—until you accomplish your goal.

# Show on Ice

The ice stadium was pitch dark as Skye and the rest of the crowd waited for the Olympic stars to enter the spotlight. Out came the gold medal winner. Her energy on the ice kept all eyes locked on her. Then the men's champion skated out. What enthusiasm he had as he danced on his skates! And he was so smooth.

But then he lost his balance, fell, and skidded across the ice. The crowd gasped. Skye was horrified with embarrassment. *Falling down in front of a few people is embarrassing enough,* she thought. *But to fall down in front of thousands would make me want to fall in a hole.*

But then, almost as fast as she could blink an eye, the skater was back up on his feet. He glided, he twirled. His skate blades flashed, and the spangles on his blue costume glittered. At the end of his beautiful performance, his skates threw up a spray of ice crystals, and he raised his arms in triumph.

The crowd roared its admiration.

## Talk About It

Why is it sometimes hard to continue doing something after you make a mistake? Name some reasons why you should continue.

# Making Dreams Come True

Colleen had always daydreamed about being a writer. She liked to put her thoughts and feelings on paper. She also liked rhyming words.

One day in school, the principal announced a fundraiser to collect money for school computers. The school would sell greeting cards. But here was the twist: the artwork and messages inside would be created by the students.

Colleen was excitied. "I'm going to do this," she told her friend Penny.

"I'll do it, too," Penny said.

Colleen began that night, but she had so many thoughts swirling through her head she couldn't catch any and put them on paper. Finally she settled on the idea of a card for getting a new pet. She worked on her poem for a couple days, then submitted it to the greeting card committee.

But her card was not chosen. At first Colleen was upset. Then she was just mad. "I know I can write good poems," she said to herself. She just needed to practice. She talked it over with Penny. Then Colleen, Penny, and their friend Wade—a classmate who also liked to write—formed a writing club. Once a week, they got together after school and read their stories and poems to one another.

Colleen and her friends improved quickly with the regular practice and each other's help. Colleen was still disappointed she hadn't won the contest, but she knew she'd be ready for the next one.

## Talk About It

Why didn't Colleen give up on writing after she didn't win the contest? What are some things you love to do so much that you won't give up on them?

# As Strong as a Blade of Grass

One spring day, Antwone was cleaning up the back porch. To his surprise he discovered a blade of grass growing in between the baseboard and the floorboards.

*What a strange place for grass to grow,* he thought to himself. *It must have taken a lot of strength for it to grow up through the foundation and right through the floor.*

That afternoon Antwone sat down to do his math homework. He rubbed his forehead as he stared at the numbers. Math was so hard for him. He erased his answer to problem number five and started over. *I hate this!* he said. *I should just give it up. I'm never going to be good at math.* It seemed like he'd been working forever at improving.

Antwone slammed his book shut.

Then he thought about the blade of grass, and he opened it again. *I need to keep pushing myself up and up and up,* he thought as he went back to working on the problems.

## Talk About It

What does Antwone learn from observing the blade of grass? Tell about a time you felt like giving up at something that was hard for you.

# Raveling and Unraveling

Sue and Bert loved to knit. They sat together at Sue's place last Saturday working their needles. "Oh, darn!" Bert said, pulling apart a row of stitches. "I screwed up this row."

"Me, too," said Sue, also unraveling a few stitches of her own. The two friends were frustrated, but kept working. Over the next half hour, they both had made a lot of progress on the scarves they were knitting. Sue was making one for her mom, Bert was making one for his little brother.

Then, Bert hit another snag. "Shoot! I hate unraveling!"

"You know what Thomas Edison said?" asked Sue, talking about the man who invented the lightbulb, the moving picture, and the record player. "After one thousand failed tries to make the lightbulb, he said to his friends, 'We're making real progress. We know a thousand ways it can't be done. We're that much closer to getting it right.' I think we should look at unraveling stitches the same way." Just as Sue was talking, she made another mistake. "Oops!" she said.

"All the craft books say there are only two stitches—knitting and purling," said Bert. "But I think there's a third stitch—unraveling, so you can start over."

## Talk About It

If Sue and Bert hate unraveling so much, why do they keep knitting? What are some other activities that take lots of practice in order to master them? What helps you keep trying?

# The Strike-Out King

"**S**trike three!" yelled the umpire and, with a sinking heart, Paul walked back to the dugout with his bat. He had struck out again.

"I think I'm the strike-out king," he told his dad that night. He tried to smile, but he was really bummed. He *always* struck out.

"If you love baseball, you can get better at it," his dad said. "You'll just have to work harder."

"I don't think I'll *ever* get better," Paul said. "No matter how hard I work."

"You know your cousin Katie?" his dad asked. "She really loves gymnastics. She wants to go to the Junior Olympics, so she's working hard at that."

"Sure, but she's great at gymnastics," Paul said. "I'm terrible at baseball."

"Well," said his dad, "she's been practicing hard at gymnasitcs for years. That's why she's good. Getting to the Junior Olympics *is* hard work. But to Katie, that work is fun."

"I do love baseball," Paul said. "Will you throw me some pitches tomorrow so I can get some practice in?"

"Sure," his dad said.

## Talk About It

Are there times when hard work is fun for you? When are they? Why are they fun?

# Problem-Solving

Life is full of problems. Being a problem-solver means you deal with problems in a positive and constructive way. You seek solutions rather than let problems get you down. You learn from mistakes, using them to find out what works.

# The Small Piece

It snowed all afternoon yesterday and all through the night. Today, the roads were clogged up and the world looked beautiful and white. And, the best news of all, school was closed! Odessa and Polly played outside until lunch. Then they went to Polly's house and, after lunch, set up a board game.

"I'll be red," Odessa and Polly said at the same time. They laughed at first, but neither girl let go of the piece.

"I'm always red," said Odessa.

"Well, it's my game," said Polly. "Why don't you be orange?"

"I *hate* orange," Odessa said. "Why don't *you* be orange?"

Polly felt the fun day slipping away as the argument heated up. Finally, she thought to herself, *This is silly. Why make a big deal about a small piece?*

"Okay," she said, "You be red. I'll be blue. Let's go."

"Thanks," Odessa said, handing Polly the dice. "Why don't you go first?"

## Talk About It

Why did Polly decide to let Odessa be red? What if they were arguing over something bigger, like what movie to see or where to go after school? Would she have given in so easily? Why or why not?

# Jeremy's Discovery

Jeremy's friends were all enjoying ice-cream cones after school. "Sure is good," Tyler said. "How come you don't get one, Jer?"

"No money," Jeremy said, pulling his pockets inside out. "Why don't you give me some of *your* ice cream?" Jeremy jokingly tried to swipe Tyler's cone from him.

"No way!" Tyler said, laughing and moving out of the way.

Jeremy could joke about it, but the truth was, he needed money. Not for big things, like a skateboard. He just wanted to get ice cream after school sometimes. And there was a new fishing magazine he'd been eyeing. His mom didn't seem to understand that chewing gum didn't cost a nickel anymore, and that a kid just needed some spending money. He tried to talk her into raising his allowance, but it was no go. And he was too young to get a *real* job. What could he do?

Jeremy thought about it while he took out the trash that afternoon, and while he was helping with dishes that night. Finally, he decided to put his worries away for the night. He crawled under the covers and spent a few minutes thinking about this situation. Finally, he fell asleep.

The next day, pouring milk over his cereal, he came up with the answer. He could go to his neighbors and ask them what they needed help with—and he'd do the work for a certain amount per job. Raking leaves, taking out garbage, whatever. To solve his money problem, he could offer solutions to other people's problems.

## Talk About It

Have you ever heard of "sleeping on" a problem to find a solution to it? Have you ever done that? What happened as a result?

# What a Mess!

Lacy's latest hobby was making jewelry. Beads in dozens of size and colors were strewn all over the bedroom: shoved in a drawer, piled on the floor, scattered in the closet. Other things messed up the room, too. Her clothes were on the floor. The bed was unmade. And the trash can was overflowing.

One day Lacy went to her room to make a necklace. She knew just the design she wanted to string up, but when she sat down to get to work she couldn't find the beads she needed. Then, looking through the mess, she stepped on a sharp clasp and yelped in pain. Sitting on the bed holding her toe, she decided her bedroom had become a problem. Maybe it wouldn't hurt to be a little more organized. She thought her mom had some shoe boxes she could use to separate her beads by color—that was a good start.

She thought more about the problem. One reason she didn't hang up her clothes was that the pole in the closet was such a stretch. She remembered a stool she had seen in the storage room. Maybe her mom would let her keep it in her room.

And the bed? She had to admit it wasn't hard to make. Maybe if she just did it first thing every morning and got it over with, it wouldn't be so bad. Just for good measure, Lacy got up right then and made the bed. Then she limped off to ask her mom for the shoe boxes and the stool.

## Talk About It

Why did Lacy make the plan to clean her room? How does it feel to discover a problem and solve it?

# Picked On

Madeline had a problem every time she rode the school bus. The line to get off moved slowly and stopped when she was right beside an older girl named Cheyenne. Every day, Cheyenne waited for Madeline and pinched her. Then Cheyenne and her friend laughed. It was embarrassing, and it hurt, too.

The first time this happened, Madeline asked her to stop, but Cheyenne just laughed and pinched her again. Madeline didn't want to tell on Cheyenne, because she lived near Cheyenne and their parents were friends. She didn't want to be a tattle-tail, especially on a family friend.

The second time Cheyenne pinched her, Madeline said, "I asked you not to do that. I don't like it." But it did no good. After the third time, Madeline had had enough. She told the bus driver.

"I'll watch for it tomorrow," the driver replied.

The next day, Madeline gave Cheyenne a warning as she approached Cheyenne's seat. "You better not pinch me today, or you're going to get in trouble."

"Yeah, right," Cheyenne said. And then she pinched Madeline.

"Cheyenne!" called the driver. "That's a behavior report."

"What?" Cheyenne said. "I didn't do anything!"

"I saw you," the driver said. "One more report and you'll be suspended from this bus."

## Talk About It

Do you think Madeline took the best steps in solving her problem? Why or why not? Was there anything you would have done differently? Do you think it's okay to report a bully? Why or why not?

# Street-Wise

Max and Donovan were members of the Fire Ants, their name for their street hockey team. With their hockey sticks over their shoulders, their skates under their arms, the boys jogged down the steps to the street.

"I'll be goalie today," Max said.

"I want to," said Donovan.

"Well, I called it first," said Max. "And you were goalie last time."

"I'm better," Donovan said. "That's why."

"I'm tired of this," Max said. "How about one of us is goalie for the first half hour and the other gets to do it for the next half hour?"

"Okay," said Donovan. "But how do we decide who gets it first?"

"Let's flip a coin," Max said, reaching into his pocket for a quarter.

"All right. Heads, I win, tails, you lose," Donovan joked.

Max laughed and flipped the coin off his thumb into the air.

## Talk About It

What does "compromise" mean? Talk about a time you compromised with a friend. How did it work out?

# Punctuality

When you are punctual you value being on time. Punctuality is a way of showing respect for others; they do not have to wait for you. Being punctual also means you meet deadlines, such as for assignments.

# Preparation for Punctuality

Al and Robby were best friends. They acted so much alike that their moms said the boys were "two peas in a pod." They both liked baseball, gaming cards, and dinosaurs. They both were good in geography. But there was one big difference between them. Al was an early bird, and Robby was always late.

One morning was worse than usual. Robby woke up late, shoved some breakfast in his mouth, and rushed down to the laundry room and back up again several times looking for clean socks and a shirt. Then he hurried to make his lunch, slathering peanut butter on his bread. "Bye, Mom!" he hollered as he ran out the door. Halfway down the block he realized he'd forgotten his English book. He slammed open the door, pounded down to his room, got the book, and ran out again. "Bye, Mom!" he hollered once more.

He arrived at school five minutes after the bell, sweating and frazzled. His mind was still rushing around. Al sat calmly next to him.

"Man, how do you do it?" Robby asked Al at recess. "You're always on time."

"I get everything ready the night before," Al said. "I make my lunch. I pack my backpack and leave it on the ledge next to the door so I can grab it on my way out. Right before bed I lay my clothes out for the next day."

"Sounds like a lot of work," Robby said.

"Nah," Al said.

## Talk About It

How do you feel when you're in a rush like Robby? How does it feel when you're late for something like school or a movie?

# The Award

Sara squirmed in her seat at the honors ceremony. The principal had just announced the attendance and punctuality awards and there, once again, was Manny, marching up to pick up his trophy. Every single year he won this award. Attendance and punctuality! Big deal.

That night, Sara was still fuming about it. "Manny gets a trophy as big as mine for math. As if being on time and at school every day is as important as being smart."

Sara's older brother shook his head. "I don't know, sounds like Manny's pretty smart, too," he said. "In college, professors will flunk you if you don't show up for enough classes. It doesn't matter how smart you are."

"Yeah, but why?" Sara huffed. "It makes no sense. I do all the work. Who cares if I'm late sometimes?"

"When you're late, you disrupt the class. You interrupt other people's learning. And if you need to ask someone to fill you in on what you missed, then you're making more work for others."

"Well, I still think being good at math is more important," Sara said.

## Talk About It

Do you agree with Sara or her brother? Why? Besides "interrupting other people's learning," what are some other reasons to be on time to class?

# Punctual Gardening

Gwen loved to work in the community garden. It was right down the block, and she spent time there after school whenever she could. Sometimes she made it every day, but sometimes she only got to the garden once a week, or not at all. She worked hard when she was there, but everything turned out scraggly—all stalk and no flowers or vegetables. Actually, her plants were pretty pitiful.

The person who had the garden spot next to her was Mr. Thurman. He had some of the same flowers and vegetables in his plot as Gwen did. But Mr. Thurman's flowers were gorgeous—plump and plentiful.

One day Gwen complained to her neighbor. "You must have one of those green thumbs," she said. "I sure don't. My flowers look awful compared to yours. Why is that?"

"I don't know," Mr. Thurman said, kneeling in the dirt. "I just followed the instructions on the seed packets. Like, I used the chart to plant the seeds at the right time for our area."

"Oh, I didn't know about that," Gwen said.

"And I water my flowers every other day," Mr. Thurman continued. "And every week I fertilize them."

"I don't get down here every day," Gwen said. "Maybe I should."

## Talk About It

Can you think of other things that need to be done on time? What are they?

# Field Trip

T.J. knew the school bus was ready to leave for its field trip to the zoo, but he knew it wouldn't leave without him. He also knew this wasn't like regular class, and being a few seconds tardy wouldn't affect his grade. So he took his time filling up his water bottle at the water fountain.

Just then, his teacher found him. "Come on, T.J.," she said. "Everyone's waiting." The two of them came out of the school, the teacher with a hand on T.J.'s shoulder. As they approached the bus, some kids laughed at him for being late.

But the adults weren't amused. "I hope we can make the science demonstration on time," one of the parent chaperones said.

"We'll probably miss the beginning," said the teacher.

"Aaaaaw!" some kids moaned when they heard that.

T.J. was quiet on the bus ride as he thought about what had happened. He had only been thinking of how his tardiness would affect himself. He hadn't thought about how being late affected everyone else.

## Talk About It

How did T.J.'s tardiness affect the others? Should he be punished for being late? Why or why not?

# The Procrastinator

The first time someone called Damon a "procrastinator," he thought he was getting a compliment. The word sounded big and important.

Then he asked his dad what it meant.

"A procrastinator is a person who puts things off until the last possible minute," his dad said.

Now that he knew what it meant, Damon could understand why he'd been called a procrastinator. He remembered lots of times he'd procrastinated in the past couple weeks. He put off doing homework one night and then had to do that instead of reading his new novel before bed. He procrastinated getting ready for the school car wash fundraiser last weekend, and ran around the house looking for the towels, washmits, and buckets he'd promised to bring. When he showed up late, everyone was waiting for him. Some cars had left without buying a wash because there weren't enough supplies to do the job.

And last week was a big one. His mom asked him several times to take the garbage to the curb, but he put it off and put it off. When he finally brought it down, the garbage truck had already passed their house. Damon and his whole family were reminded of his procrastinating habit all week long—whenever they went in the garage and smelled the week-old trash.

## Talk About It

Why do you think people procrastinate? Is it okay to procrastinate if you eventually get things done? Why or why not? Name some problems that can be caused by procrastination.

# Relationships with Others

Part of having strong character is having strong relationships with your family and friends. These relationships grow strong when you put effort into them: you *build* relationships by contributing your time, kindness, and honest feelings. It's also important to recognize the relationships you have and be grateful for them. You can show you're grateful by making a point to spend time with your family and friends and by respecting them.

# For the Love of the Game

Ernie dribbled the ball. He passed it to Finn, who made a move to avoid an imaginary defender and dribbled toward the basket. Finn did a pump fake and then threw it in.

"Two points!" Ernie cried. "Too bad it's not this easy when all the guys are here."

A few minutes later, the guys began to show up to the court, and they started a game. Ernie and Finn were captains. The boys played hard, charging for loose balls, racing to both ends of the court, laying in tough shots. Both teams wanted to win badly, but no referee was needed because the game was good-natured. Everyone had fun.

The game was neck and neck. After about an hour, each team had scored 32 points and it was about time to go home for dinner. "Next shot wins," Finn said. Ernie scooped a bounce pass from his teammate, dribbled near the free throw line, and shot the winning basket.

"Game over!" he shouted. His whole team hooted with excitement.

"Ah, man!" Finn said as he kicked the gravel. But then he called out to the other team, "Great game, guys! See you tomorrow."

"Yeah, good game, Finn," Ernie said. "I'll be here tomorrow."

## Talk About It

Why is it sometimes hard to have fun when you lose? Is it easier or harder to have fun if your opponents are good friends? Why? If you had to choose, which is more important—winning or having fun with friends? Why?

# The Next One's for Us

Tanisha and Sandy had been working together for two weeks on an art project for school—a colorful jungle scene in a cardboard box. At first, Sandy didn't think she'd like working on the jungle project. It sounded like a lot of work, and she wasn't very good at art. But working with Tanisha turned out to be great.

First, they brainstormed what to make and how to make it. Then they phoned and emailed each other for a couple days to iron out details and share new ideas. And then, of course, they spent hours working together sketching, cutting, coloring, and pasting.

Now the work finally was done. The two girls sat together, staring at the scene they had worked on so hard. They'd done a terrific job and, although they'd been friends before they began, they were even closer now.

"It's kind of a bummer to be done with this," Sandy said, still looking at the jungle scene.

Tanisha nodded in agreement. "I know," she said. "Let's think of another project. But we'll make this one for us—not for school."

Sandy's face lit up, and the two girls immediately began to discuss what their next creation would be.

## Talk About It

Why did working on the jungle project make Sandy and Tanisha's friendship stronger? Why do you think they want to do another project together?

# A New Holiday Tradition

Jay and his sister, Tahira, were excited. It was December 26, the beginning of the Kwanzaa holiday. Although this African-American holiday was started many years ago, this was the first time Jay and Tahira's family was celebrating it. They were excited to begin a new tradition of celebrating their family and their culture.

Jay helped his mom arrange the table where their family would gather every evening for seven days. On the table was a straw mat, which symbolized the importance of tradition. An ear of corn and a candleholder with seven candles were on the mat. The corn symbolized children and the future. Each candle stood for a traditional African value. Tahira, Jay, and their dad made the candleholder themselves from a piece of tree limb that had fallen into their yard.

With a hush, the children gathered at the table. Their dad lit the first candle.

"This candle stands for unity," he said, pointing to it. "This is an important idea for us and our ancestors. What do you think of when you hear the word *unity*?"

Tahira beamed. That was easy. "Our family," she said.

## Talk About It

What are some special celebrations, ceremonies, or traditions you share with your family? Why do you do them? How do traditions help strengthen relationships?

# The Blanket

Nate dragged his blanket to the couch, where he curled up inside it to watch TV with his mom and brother. Otis smiled at Nate in his colorful wrap. "Wish I had a big *blankey*," Otis said in a sing-song voice, teasing him.

Their mother heard the comment, and she set Otis straight.

"Nate's blanket isn't just a thing to him. It's something that makes him feel safe. It makes him feel peaceful inside. I would think you would understand that. Isn't that how you feel when you're writing?"

"I guess," Otis said, laughing. "But I don't carry my computer and work on my blog everywhere I go!"

"Maybe you would if you could," his mother responded. "Instead, you carry the feeling. You think about what you might write in your blog, even when you're not at the computer. Nate is little and hasn't yet learned that he can have those good feelings without his blanket."

## Talk About It

What are some things that make your family members feel safe, peaceful, or just plain good? What can you do to show you respect their needs?

# The Piano Recital

Gretchen and Jalen had been best friends for years. They loved playing duets on the piano in the music room at school. When they began taking piano lessons with the school music teacher, he found them lots of other duets to learn.

For their school's winter concert, Jalen was chosen to play the piano part. Gretchen was really disappointed she didn't get chosen for the part. At first she complained to her mom that it wasn't fair. She was as good as Jalen! She moped around for a few days. But when she saw how excited Jalen was, she started to get excited, too.

When it was time for the concert, Gretchen was in the front row. "This is going to be so cool," she told her parents as they waited for the lights to go down. "I can't wait to see Jalen perform and hear the new pieces he learned."

The crowd hushed as the lights dimmed in the cafeteria and one spotlight beamed onto Jalen. Gretchen was filled with pride as she listened to him play. He was great!

After the show Gretchen found her friend near the stage and told him how excellent the performance was. "I loved it," she said.

"Thanks!" Jalen said to Gretchen. "It was kind of scary but also super fun."

## Talk About It

Why was it hard at first for Gretchen to be happy for Jalen? What helped her be able to enjoy his success?

# Relationship with Self

When you have a good relationship with yourself you are comfortable with being you, you try to understand who you are, and you have things you like to do alone. Having positive feelings about your talents and skills strengthens your relationship with yourself.

# Good at This and That

Keith was an average student in elementary school. He didn't particularly like sports. On the other hand, his older brother Jason was a straight-A student. He was also on his middle school's cross country and basketball teams. Teachers and friends often had great things to say about Jason's grades and athletic skills. And people who came over *always* commented on the big cross country trophy Jason had in the living room.

Keith liked and admired his brother a lot, and he knew Jason deserved all the nice things people said. But hearing those comments only reminded Keith that he wasn't as good at them. It used to be hard to accept how different he and Jason were.

But then Keith thought about it, and he realized there were things he was talented at, too. For one thing, he was an excellent writer, and he also was a good rapper. Keith loved to write and perform his own raps, and people who heard them said he had a way with words and rhythm. After he realized that, the differences with his brother didn't bother him anymore. In fact, Keith made up a little rap about their differences:

I'm good at this,
Jason's good at that.
We both have things
We're very good at.

## Talk About It

Why was it hard for Keith to see his own talents? What do you think helped him recognize his own special abilities? What are your talents?

# Dolls

**M**aggie brought her dolls to Tess's house Saturday morning, just like she and her friends always did. Sitting in Tess's room, Maggie took her dolls out of her bag. "You guys want to play?" she asked.

"I don't think so," Tess said. "Dolls are for babies."

"Yeah, I didn't even bring any," said Beatrix.

The other girls agreed. They wanted to talk about boys and makeup. Maggie sat with her friends and tried to enjoy herself, but she wasn't very interested in those things. It sounded a lot more fun to play like kids. In fact, it felt a little lonely to think she didn't have as much in common with her friends anymore. They'd been playing dolls together since kindergarten.

Maggie went home that afternoon and played outside with her little sister. They raked the autumn leaves into the shape of a house with three rooms and played there until supper time. When she went to bed that night, a doll was in her arms.

## Talk About It

Do you think Maggie should start doing the things her friends are doing so she can stay close to them? Why or why not?

# Diary to Grandpa

Filipe lay in bed all day long. Ever since the call came that Grandpa died, Filipe didn't want to see anyone.

Sometimes he cried a little. Sometimes he got angry at everyone: at the doctor for not saving his grandfather, at all the people visiting and talking so loudly, even at Grandpa. They had planned a trip to the science museum. Now the only trip would be to the funeral home.

Later that day, Filipe's dad came in and sat down on the bed. Filipe talked about all of his feelings and his dad listened.

"You're grieving," his dad said when Filipe was done talking. "These mixed feelings happen when a person grieves." Filipe was relieved to know these feelings were normal. "I remember when my mom died. I was furious at everybody," his dad went on. "One reason I felt so bad is because I was afraid I hadn't let her know how much I loved her. I wrote a lettter to her about it, and that made me feel better."

Filipe perked up for the first time all day. He loved to write. He kept a journal and wrote in it about bugs he identified and places he had fished. The thought of writing to Grandpa appealed to Filipe. He could have a "Diary to Grandpa." He could write in it for as long as he wanted to.

## Talk About It

Filipe loved to write. What is something that you love to do? How could you use it to help you get through hard times?

# The Model Airplane

Akashi's friends stopped by his house and they were all talking on the porch. It was a blistering hot summer day. The guys were going to the mall to hang out, and they wanted Akashi to join them. "Come on, Akashi," Justin said. "It's so hot out. It'll feel nice and cool inside the mall."

Akashi thought of his model airplane arranged on the floor in the other room. The fuselage and tail were finished. He just had to add the wings and then the details, like the propellers, the pilot, and the wheels. The mall sounded fun, but working on the model sounded more fun. "Thanks for asking me, but I'm going to stay home," he said.

"I heard there's a new climbing wall at the sports store," said Malik. "Let's check it out!"

Usually Akashi would hang out with the guys in a heartbeat. They were great friends. But today he felt more like working on his airplane. After he finished putting it together he would paint on the stripes. When it was dry, he would use wire to hang it from the ceiling in his bedroom so it looked like it was flying among the other planes there. "Sorry, guys. Have fun, but I'm going to finish this cargo plane I started."

## Talk About It

If you were Akashi, would you have gone with the guys to the mall? Why or why not? Why is it important to have a hobby or special interest just for yourself?

# Sophie's Summer

After the last day of elementary school, Sophie looked ahead to middle school. There would be lots of opportunities to join clubs and sports teams. The more she thought about it, the more she wanted to run on the track team. So Sophie made herself a promise. She would practice hard all summer to try to make the middle school track team in the fall.

She stretched her muscles and warmed up each morning with some jumping jacks. Then she chose her route. Some days she ran by the lake, startling the Canada geese. Sometimes she ran in the woods, hearing the pine straw crunch under her feet. At first she couldn't run very far. It just wore her out, and she wondered if she wanted to be on the track team after all. But each week she ran a little bit farther. Soon, she started doing quick sprints, too.

Sophie ran and ran. And every day after showering, she took out a notebook and wrote down where and how far she ran.

Soon Sophie's daily run was so much a part of her summer and her life that she couldn't imagine not doing it. She decided that even if she didn't make the track team, she was going to keep running—just because she enjoyed herself.

## Talk About It

Why do you think Sophie liked to run so much? What are some activities you enjoy doing by yourself?

# Respect for the Environment

When you have respect for the environment you honor nature. You are grateful for the earth and show it by treating it well. You do your part to keep the land, water, and air clean and protected.

# Environmentalists

Gabby, Ed, and their mom looked at the bagfuls of aluminum cans and plastic water bottles. In another corner of the barn lay sloppy stacks of newspapers. "I'm sure those are full of roaches," their mom said. "This recycling stuff sure is a pain in the neck."

They lived outside of town on a farm, where no recycling trucks came, so if the family wanted to recycle they had to do it themselves. They had to collect, separate, and bag the recycling, just like people in the city. But then they had to pile it into the car and drive it to the recycling center 22 miles away.

"We may have to go back to no recycling," their mom said. "We may have to start throwing everything away in the garbage."

Then she glanced up. Two pairs of eyes were gazing at her in horror.

"Mom, there's a hole in the ozone layer that's bigger than Europe," Gabby said. "If we recycle cans and bottles, less fuel is burned to make new ones, and the hole doesn't grow as fast."

"Every second, one acre of tropical rain forest is cut down," said Ed. "If we recycle paper, fewer trees are cut down."

"It really makes a difference, Mom," added Gabby.

"Wow, you really feel strongly about this," their mom said. "Okay, then. You're right. But I'll need your help."

The siblings glanced at each other with relief. "Of course, Mom," said Ed.

## Talk About It

Why do you think recycling is so important to Ed and Gabby? Does your family recycle? Why or why not?

# Nature in My Neighborhood

Annika got out of school and hurried home, ate a quick snack, and then ran to the city park nearby. Sometimes she played red rover or hide-and-seek with her friends in the neighborhood, but today she played alone, and that was fine, too. She climbed up a maple tree, feeling the rough bark on her skin. She perched on a limb and looked down at the younger kids on the slides and swings.

Later, near the pond, she tried to catch a frog as it flopped through the high grass and into the water. On her way back home she stopped at a red light and noticed that one of the neighborhood stores had a windowbox full of flowers. She walked over to see what was growing in them.

Annika liked all the seasons—kicking through red leaves in the fall, making snow forts in winter, and in the spring she loved seeing new flowers blooming all along the boulevard and in the parks. And, of course, summer was the best of all. She loved the water. Her favorite summer activity was walking to the pond with her older sister for a swim.

In bed that night, Annika planned out a new route to walk to school the next day. She'd noticed a bird's nest under the eaves at the library last week, and she wanted to make sure it was still there and see if any eggs had hatched yet. She was sure she'd be able to hear the baby birds chirping.

## Talk About It

How is nature a part of your daily routine? Where do you most often notice nature?

# Wildflowers

"Here's my favorite wildflower," Ryan's stepmom said. She pointed out several tiny white flowers with glossy leaves. They were walking through a park, enjoying one of the first really warm days of spring. Summer was on its way, and Ryan was excited. "It's called 'trailing arbutus.' It's the first flower out every spring."

But Ryan wasn't listening. He was peeling bark off a tree.

"Hey, you shouldn't do that," his stepmom said.

"But it's already starting to peel," Ryan said. It was hard to resist finishing the job. Then he noticed some bright red flowers off the path. "Whoa, look at that!" he said, trudging toward them.

"Ryan!" said his stepmom. "Please be careful. It's wrong to step on flowers and destroy trees—even if the bark is starting to peel. It's great that you appreciate nature, but the first rule of nature is to leave it as you found it."

"Can I at least pick some flowers?" Ryan said, bending over to touch the red ones he'd found. He was thinking about taking some home and putting them in a vase with the trailing arbutus his stepmom liked.

But she shook her head. "If you pick them, they'll die and there will be fewer of them for others to enjoy. Some wildflowers have disappeared completely because people picked them all. But if you let them be, they'll spread."

## Talk About It

Why do you think Ryan's stepmom said the first rule of nature is to leave it as you found it?

# A Web Instinct

Edwin and his dad were fascinated watching the big spider build its web in a bush in the backyard. Edwin looked closely at the wispy strands of white—they looked like fine thread.

"How does the spider know what strands to put the sticky stuff on and which ones not to?" Edwin asked his dad. "And then how does it know not to step on the ones that are sticky?"

"Instinct," his dad said.

"What do you mean?"

"Instinct is like an a built-in sense that helps all animals know how to do whatever they need to do," said his dad. "The instinct that helps the spider stay off the sticky strands is similar to the instinct that guides birds to fly south in the winter and causes animals to grow thicker fur for cold weather. You could even say there's instinct in a seed that lets it know whether to grow into a watermelon or a tomato."

"I never thought about animals and plants having instinct like people do," Edwin said. "I like that."

## Talk About It

Can you think of other examples of instinct in nature? What are they?

# Preserving Butterflies

"Look at that beautiful red plant," said Margie's Uncle Paul. Just as he pointed to the plant, something even more beautiful landed on Uncle Paul's finger: a butterfly with brown- and red-striped wings.

"Wow," Margie said. "That's awesome."

She and Uncle Paul spent the entire afternoon at the butterfly garden, watching 50 different kinds of butterflies color the air. Margie was surprised and saddened to learn that some of the kinds of butterflies they'd seen were in danger of dying out.

The next week, Uncle Paul took Margie to the library where she checked out a book on how to make her own butterfly garden. She read about what kinds of butterflies were endangered in their part of the world, and how she could help support them. After she'd done all her research, she planted the brightly flowering plants the book recommended along a fence in her uncle's backyard.

Before long, the plants were doing their job: attracting those endangered butterlies. They were pretty to look at, but more important, all the flowers Margie planted gave the butterflies a much-needed place to feed and reproduce.

## Talk About It

What does *endangered* mean? What are some endangered plants, animals, or insects you know about? What can people do to help them?

# Respect for Others

Having respect for others means thinking of them as important people. When you respect others you accept them for who they are—including their faults. You try to understand people's needs and you show them courtesy. You show concern for their thoughts, feelings, and beliefs. You do not have to agree with people to respect them.

# Very Private

Trisha and Mario's mom gave them both journals as gifts. The cover of Trisha's was a deep blue and Mario's was a steel gray. Both books had locks on them. Their mom talked about the importance of journaling. She told them their thoughts and feelings were special.

Mario and Trisha both enjoyed writing in their journals. They loved having a place to write down what was on their minds. Each day they made sure they locked the books and put them away.

One morning Mario was walking down the hall to fix his breakfast when he stopped suddenly. There, on Trisha's bed, was her open journal. She was taking a shower to get ready for school and had forgotten to put it away.

He thought about all the private information he could find and use to tease and laugh at his sister. The temptation to read it was almost too much.

He stood in the doorway looking at the journal.

Then he let out a big sigh and continued on to the kitchen. Eating cereal and bananas, he kept thinking about the journal. It was so inviting, and he was *so* curious.

But he knew it was important to respect a person's privacy. He also thought of how bad it would be if Trisha read *his* journal. To avoid temptation, he decided to stay in the kitchen until Trisha was back in her room.

## Talk About It

Why did Mario want to read his sister's journal? Why did he decide not to? Think of a time when someone looked at something of yours that was private. How did you feel? Why is it important to respect people's privacy?

# Agreeing to Disagree

"George, I just can't stand to watch that movie one more time," Emma complained. "We've watched it about five Saturdays in a row."

"Just three," George said. "But I love the special effects. You'll get into it once it starts." He pushed in the tape.

That made Emma angrier. "I'm going home," she said, getting up to go.

Later, lying on her bed, Emma felt unsettled. She tried to read a book, but kept reading the same line over and over. All she could think of was her fight with George. It was not a bad fight, as fights go. Neither one insulted the other or said anything mean. Still, Emma felt uncomfortable.

George called a little while later. "Let's talk about this some more," he said.

"I'm sorry I walked out on you," Emma said.

"I'm sorry for trying to make you watch the movie again," George said. "We don't have to watch it anymore."

"We can watch it *sometimes*," Emma said. "Just not every weekend."

"Even if it is the greatest movie ever?" George asked jokingly.

"It is *not* the greatest movie ever," Emma said. "But even though we disagree, we can still be friends."

## Talk About It

Why is it sometimes uncomfortable to disagree with a friend? When friends disagree, what can they do to make sure they remain friends?

# Alike but Different

Crystal stared at the two new girls in her class—they were twins. She was fascinated. They looked exactly alike: long brown curly hair pulled back in ponytails, dark eyes, and the same skin tone. They were even the same size. Crystal thought it would be hard to have another person exactly like you in the world.

*Thank goodness they're dressed differently,* she thought to herself. *Otherwise I wouldn't be able to tell them apart.*

As the week wore on, she began to notice differences between the twins. Kasandra was great at softball, but Rhonda had a hard time hitting the ball and she didn't like to run. Rhonda was quiet. She always had a book with her so she could catch a few pages of reading if she had some down time. Kasandra was outgoing and liked to be with friends all the time. Once Crystal noticed these differences, she could tell the sisters walked and talked a little differently, too. They even each had a unique way of looking at you when you talked.

Saturday after the first week of school was over, Crystal talked to her mom about the twins. "The first day I couldn't tell them apart," she said. "Now, they don't even have to be together for me to know who's who. They're really different people."

## Talk About It

When you first meet people, what kinds of judgements do you make about them? Why is it important to get to know people?

# The Love Note

In school one morning, Jim wrote a "love note" to Dena—but he signed it from Sander, not from himself. He carefully folded it and asked Sander to hand it to Dena.

*This is going to be really funny,* he thought.

Dena read the note and looked away, embarrassed. After class she walked with Sander to lunch. "Sander," she said, "you're a good friend, but let's keep it at that, nothing more, okay?" Jim walked behind them giggling to himself.

"What?" Sander asked, but Dena was already walking away.

Jim sat next to Sander on the bus ride home. As soon as he sat, he burst out laughing and confessed about the note. "Oh, man, that was hilarious!" he said.

To his surprise Sander was really upset. "Not funny," Sander said. "Not funny at all!"

"Oh, come on," Jim said. "It was a great joke!"

"Not to me!" he said. "Now I'll be embarrassed whenever I'm around Dena. How would you feel if someone did that to you?"

Jim was silent for the rest of the trip home. He hadn't meant to hurt his friend. He just wanted to have fun.

"I'm sorry for the note," Jim said to his friend before he got off the bus.

"You better tell Dena what you did, too," Sander replied.

"Okay," Jim said.

## Talk About It

Jim didn't expect Sander to be so upset by his trick—why not? Why *was* Sander so upset?

# Super Smart

**M**ary and her friends were standing on the playground when Christine came up. "Hey, ugly!" she yelled at Mary. "You're the ugliest person I ever saw. What do you think about that?"

Mary knew Christine was just looking for a fight. She also knew if she called Christine a name back—or acted angry about being called ugly—Christine would take the chance to start one. So Mary tried something different. "Okay," she said. "Whatever."

"U-u-u-u-gly!" Christine said.

"Yep," Mary said. Christine stood there for a few seconds, then she walked away.

When she was gone, Mary's friends congratulated her. "You're super smart," Wes said. "You left her with nothing else to say."

"You're the one who aces all the English tests," Mary said to Wes. "You're the super-smart one."

"But Mary, that really was smart," Val said. "Great way to avoid a fight."

"There are lots of ways to be smart," Wes said. "Look at Val. He can get even the bossiest person in the school to stop and listen. He's smart at dealing with people."

Val laughed. "Yes, thank you very much," he said. "I'm a genius at talking."

## Talk About It

Do you know people who are "super smart" at certain things? Give some examples. Have you ever told these people that you respect their particular talent?

# Respect for Self

Having respect for yourself means you think of yourself as an important person. You take care of yourself by eating a healthy diet, getting enough rest and exercise, and avoiding risky or dangerous behavior. You don't let friends pressure you into doing things you don't want to do. When you respect yourself, you understand better how to respect others.

# Forgiving Myself

Lori and Erin were inline skating at the roller rink and having a great time. When their favorite song came on, they skated faster, feeling really hyper. Colorful lights swept across the floor. Then the DJ announced it was time for the hokey-pokey. As usual the first three kids who reached the middle of the rink could lead the dance.

Lori pushed Erin aside and raced to the middle. Erin fell down as two other kids arrived at the center with Lori. Erin was furious. When the music began, she tried to enjoy the hokey-pokey, but she couldn't stop thinking about how her friend pushed her. Her face burned with anger. After the dance, she raced up to Lori.

"You knew I wanted to lead this time," she yelled at Lori. "But you pushed me down so you could get ahead of me."

"I did not push you down!"

"You did, too!" Erin screamed. Then she noticed that kids all around were staring at her. Embarrassed, she skated off to the restroom to cool down. She splashed water on her face until she felt calmer. Then she looked at herself in the mirror and thought about what happened. "Why did I get so upset?" she said to her reflection. "What a dork I am."

Sipping a lemonade at the snack bar gave her even more time to think. *I really made a fool of myself,* she thought. *Lori will probably never want to be my friend again.* On the car ride home, both Erin and Lori were quiet.

continued →

## Forgiving Myself (continued)

That night, Erin was still thinking about how she had acted and how bad it felt. But then she thought of some of the embarrassing things Lori and her other friends had done. Erin didn't keep reminding them of their mistakes, and she didn't tease them. And she always forgave her friends when they did things that made her mad. She realized she was being harder on herself than she was on others, and she decided not to keep criticizing herself for what she did. Then she called Lori and apologized for yelling at her.

"I'm sorry, too," Lori said. "I didn't mean to push you. I just got excited."

## Talk About It

Why do you think Erin was hard on herself? Is it hard to forgive yourself for your mistakes? Why or why not?

# Hanging Out with the Big Guys

Ramón was glad to meet the new, older kids Niko had been hanging out with. They were funny and joked a lot. He was having a good time until a couple of the guys pulled out cigarettes. Ramón was shocked to see his buddy Niko take one, light it up, and begin smoking.

Niko handed the cigarette to Ramón, but Ramón waved it away. "No thanks," he said, feeling uncomfortable.

"Come on," Niko said, pushing the cigarette back toward Ramón. Then he leaned over and whispered. "You don't have to inhale, just puff on it. We're hanging out with the big guys now."

The other boys began to tease Ramón.

"You a mama's boy?" one asked. "Or just a sissy?"

"Nobody's looking," Niko said emphatically. "Just try it."

"Sorry, guys. See you later," Ramón replied. And he walked home by himself.

## Talk About It

Why do you think Niko pressured Ramón to smoke? If you were in Ramón's position, would it be hard to say no? Why or why not?

# Talking to Myself

B rady stood in his room looking at the scratched and ruined CDs on the floor. "You're so stupid," he yelled. "That's the dumbest thing you've ever done. All you do is mess things up!"

When he walked into the kitchen for dinner, his mom stopped him. "Who were you yelling at in there?" she asked. "That's a terrible way to treat your friends. And *what* were you so upset about?"

Brady was a little surprised that she heard him. "Oh, I left some CDs out of their cases on the floor, and then when I wasn't looking I stepped on them and scratched a couple."

"So you yelled at your friends?" his mom asked, sitting at the table.

"I wasn't talking to any friends," Brady said. "I was talking to myself. I wouldn't talk to a friend that way."

"You'd talk to yourself that way but not a friend?"

"Right. It would be mean to treat a friend like that," Brady said.

"Well, you're still being mean to someone," said his mom.

## Talk About It

Is it okay to be mean to yourself? Why or why not? Is it okay to be *mad* at yourself? What are some positive things you can do when you're mad at yourself?

# Four Eyes

**M**onique was nervous about wearing her new glasses at school, so she kept them in her book bag until the last minute. When reading began, she slipped them on. Brandon saw them immediately.

"Hey, four eyes," he chided. He poked the other kids around them, to make sure everyone saw the glasses. Kids giggled and made insults. At recess, kids teased her even more, even though she left them in her desk.

"How are the new glasses working out?" her dad asked that night.

"I can't wear them anymore," Monique said in a disgusted voice. "I hate them and the kids call me 'four eyes.' These glasses are not going to ruin my school year."

Her dad listened. Then he reminded Monique of the headaches she got when reading before she had the glasses. "Your health is more important than some comments from kids at school," he said.

Monique knew her dad was right, even though she didn't think he understood how hard it was to be teased. She wore her glasses all that evening, and she looked at herself each time she walked by the mirror. She looked okay, she thought. Actually, she looked pretty stylish. She got her homework done quicker than usual that night, and with fewer mistakes. And afterward her eyes didn't feel the least bit strained. She didn't have a headache. Lying in bed that night, she thought about the kids at school. She had a big decision to make.

## Talk About It

Do you think Monique will wear the glasses to school tomorrow? Why or why not? How would you decide if you were Monique?

# Speaking Up

Charlotte was an excellent lip reader. The hearing impairment she was born with made it a necessity. She almost never missed a word when someone was talking to her. But communicating back to the person could be a problem.

Charlotte and her family used sign language with great speed, and Charlotte had a good friend who learned to use it, too. But when she was with people who didn't understand signing, Charlotte was stuck. She had to rely on someone else to speak for her or write down what she wanted to say.

When Charlotte was in third grade, her family moved to a town that had an oral school for the hearing impaired. There, Charlotte began learning how to sound out words. It was a lot of hard work learning to use her vocal chords.

Although it took a lot of time and effort, she kept on. She was determined to learn to speak orally. She had a lot of ideas to express.

## Talk About It

Does Charlotte respect herself? How can you tell? How does working to express yourself add to your self-respect?

# Responsibility

Responsibility means knowing what is expected of you and doing it. When people are responsible, they work hard to do everything they are supposed to. Responsible people are trustworthy and reliable. Knowing others can depend on them makes them feel confident and positive about themselves.

213

# Handling Money

One afternoon Awan was talking to his friend Travis, who had just bought a fancy new remote-control car. "How can you afford that?" Awan asked. "Your allowance is the same as mine." His own allowance always seemed to disappear before the end of the week.

"My dad taught me a system for handling money," Travis answered. "It's called the 'spend some, save some, give some away system.'"

"Sounds high tech," Awan said, smiling. But he wanted to learn the system, so he listened while Travis explained it. Awan decided to try it.

That Friday when he got his allowance he put one-third of it in an envelope to deposit in his savings account. That was the "save some" part. For the "give some away" part, he put one-third in a box on the convenience store counter that went toward research on childhood diseases. He knew his mom gave money to that organization—she said it really helped. The rest of his allowance was Awan's to do with whatever he wanted: the "spend some" part.

When Awan bought gum or other things that week, he had to be more careful than before. There wasn't as much money to spend. But Awan didn't mind. It felt good to know some money was in the bank, and it felt even better to know he'd helped an important cause.

Awan did the same thing with his allowance the next week, and again the week after that. Within a few months, he had a decent amount saved up, which he planned to spend on a skateboard.

## Talk About It

Do you think it was hard for Awan to stick with the "spend some, save some, give some away system"? Why or why not? Would it be hard for you? Explain.

# The Audition

**M**adison was auditioning for the lead role in the school play. She was a good actor and was doing well on her tryout—until she saw Ms. Johnson, the teacher who was directing the play, frowning and waving a hand by her face. Madison thought she looked as if she couldn't wait for her to finish. When she saw her, she forgot her next line and stammered.

Afterward, Madison knew she had blown it. "Ms. Johnson knew she wasn't going to give me the part even before I was done," she said to herself. "I'm sure I won't get it, because she made me mess up."

When the list of parts was posted the next day, Madison didn't even want to look at it. She knew it wouldn't be good news. And it wasn't. The part she tried out for went to Harriet.

"I knew you didn't like my tryout," Madison said when she saw Ms. Johnson that day. "During the audition, you were waving at me to hurry up. You made me forget my line."

At first, Ms. Johnson was puzzled. Then she said, "Oh, Madison, a bug was flying around my head. I'm sorry if I distracted you, but I didn't *make* you forget your line."

Later, after Madison had gotten over being upset, she realized Ms. Johnson was right. She was responsible for messing up her lines, not Ms. Johnson.

## Talk About It

Do you agree that Ms. Johnson did not make Madison forget her lines? Why or why not? What lesson has Madison learned?

# The Big Eraser

Kendra made a mistake on her math test and picked up the large pink eraser on her desk. The eraser was bigger than her calculator, and on top of it were the words, "For Big Mistakes." Kendra knew she could never use up all of that gigantic eraser. But sometimes, like now, as she rubbed out the wrong figures on her test, it felt like she really did need such a big one. Last week she made so many errors on her math homework that she erased holes in the sheet of paper.

After school that day she was so happy to have the test behind her she felt hyper. She was so filled with energy that she started to play tag with her sister—inside—and before long they knocked over a picture frame and broke it.

Their mom was really angry. "I've told you many times not to run indoors," she said.

"I'm sorry, Mom," said Kendra. "I made a mistake—a big one." She thought about her big eraser, and wished she could use it to erase mistakes in life, too, not just in math. *That would make life a lot easier,* she thought.

"Well," said her mom, "what do you think we should do about the broken frame?"

Kendra thought for a minute. She couldn't erase her mistake, but she could make up for it.

## Talk About It

What are some ways Kendra can make up for breaking the picture frame? Does being responsible mean never making mistakes? What's the responsible thing to do when you make mistakes?

# Wash and Wear

Bennie was reading his science book in class when he looked down and discovered his socks didn't match. One was dark blue and one was black. By his bedroom lamp that morning he couldn't tell, but under the bright classroom lights the difference was obvious.

That night he complained to his mother about it. "I looked like a geek, Mom!" he said. "I wish you'd pay more attention when you're folding my laundry."

His mom put down the papers she'd been reading for work. "You know," she said, "I have a lot of things to do, and *your* laundry is only one of them. Instead of complaining, maybe you could thank me for doing it."

Bennie thought about it, and he decided she was right. In fact, her birthday was coming up, and he had a great idea for a gift: he could do his own laundry.

So Bennie asked his mom to teach him. She showed him how to separate the colors, choose the right water temperature, and not to put too many clothes in a load. Bennie learned the hard way that if he put off folding his clothes too long, they'd be all wrinkled. And that red colors sometimes turned his other clothes pink. For a while, matching socks was the least of Bennie's problems. But he soon got the hang of it. Then one day, his mother thanked *him*. "Taking responsibility for your own laundry makes things easier for me, Bennie. Thank you."

## Talk About It

What responsibilities do you have at home? What others could you take on?

# Dalmatian Creation

Nick was drawing with markers one afternoon with his white dog Frosty flopped down next to him. Suddenly Nick had an idea. He took a black marker and drew a dot on Frosty. The dog didn't seem to mind, and Nick liked the way it looked. So he added another dot, and then another. Before long, Frosty was as polka-dotted as a Dalmatian.

But when Nick brought the dog into the kitchen to show his parents, they *did* mind. "What happened to Frosty?" his dad asked.

Nick's mom saw the marker in his hand and said, "I hope you used a washable marker! Those spots are going to be hard to get out. And guess who's going to do it."

Nick's mom was right—they were hard to get out. Nick lifted Frosty into the bathtub for a hot, sudsy wash. The dog didn't like being in there and kept trying to get away, but Nick held him steady. Water sloshed all over the floor. After the bath, though, the spots remained and Nick heaved Frosty into the tub again. Even after four baths, Frosty's coat looked grey. The family took him to a dog groomer, who was able to get him clean using a harsh wash. Poor Frosty's skin turned red and welty. The groomer put a medicated rinse on the dog to relieve the welts.

Nick felt awful that Frosty went through so much discomfort, so he gave the dog extra attention and love over the next few weeks.

## Talk About It

Did Nick behave in a responsible way in this story? If so, when? If not, what could he do to be more responsible?

# Self-Discipline

When you have self-discipline you do what you know you should and don't do what you should not. You have the self-control to learn difficult new skills and cut out bad habits. You have good control of your actions and words, and you don't act on bad thoughts. (For example, if someone says something mean to you, you don't say something mean back, even if you think it might feel good to say it.)

# Keeping Cool in School

Kasib and his whole class sat in the classroom with the lights off and their heads down. Outside, Kasib could hear other kids shouting and running around during recess. It made him really mad that the teacher was punishing the whole class just because a few kids wouldn't be quiet during reading time. He was glad when school was over, because he didn't think he could hold in his anger much longer.

Even when Kasib got home, he was still mad. To release all the anger in his system, he decided to get some exercise. He called his friend Andy to join him for a game of tennis at the park. Whacking the ball across the net and running around the court to make shots really helped him release that built-up energy.

"I thought I was going to explode today at school," Kasib said to his friend between games. "I felt like standing up and yelling at my teacher, 'You're not being fair!' But I knew that wasn't a very good idea."

"Yep," Andy said. "That would've been a bad idea all right."

"I'd probably still be in detention," said Kasib, laughing.

"One time I got really mad at school," Andy said. "I was in the classroom so I couldn't run around to burn off the anger. So I made a fist under my desk and pretended I was filling it up with all my anger. When it was full, I just opened my hand and let the anger float away."

"That sounds a lot smarter than yelling at the teacher," Kasib said.

## Talk About It

Think of a time you "lost your cool" when you were angry. How did you feel afterward? What are some things you can do to control your anger?

# The DVD

Jennifer rounded the aisle of the store when she saw it: the DVD she had been wanting. It was the one everyone at school was talking about.

She looked over her shoulder. No one else was around. She had her bag with her, and the door was near by. Jennifer *knew* she could easily slide the DVD into her bag and walk out, and no one would ever know.

Jennifer fingered the DVD, trying to calm herself down. She really wanted it. She felt like her heart was jumping out of her chest. What if she got caught? What would her parents think? What about her friends?

Jennifer decided to take a moment to think. She wandered over to another department and looked at socks, then at shoes. Walking up and down the aisles, she talked to herself about stealing. What if she went to jail? Her parents would have to come and get her. They might not trust her again for a long time.

Then Jennifer thought about what would happen if she stole the DVD—and *didn't* get caught. What would that mean?

Jennifer took a deep breath and decided to get out of the store— without the DVD.

## Talk About It

What might have happened if Jennifer stole the DVD and got away with it? Why do you think she decided not to steal it?

# Carried Away with Reading

Russell was a bright kid, but he struggled with reading. He worked hard, and he was improving, but he wanted to do better. When the school year ended, his teacher recommended that he practice reading every day over the summer to improve his skills.

Russell thought that was a good idea, so the first Saturday of the summer he and his dad went to the library. They selected several short books for Russell to read that week. His favorite subjects were ocean life and the weather, and he was fascinated with storms, especially those that started at sea. So he grabbed a book on hurricanes, one on tsunamis, and one on the water cycle. He also loved to read books that were funny, so he added a joke book to his stack.

Russell worked out a schedule to read several times during the day. He thought 15 minutes was a good amount of time. He would read right after breakfast, lunch, and dinner.

Russell ate lunch when he and his dad got home from the library, and then he started on his reading schedule. He borrowed him mom's kitchen timer and set it for 15 minutes. At first it was difficult to concentrate for so long. He read slowly as he sounded out new words. He thought the timer would never go off.

Russell read for 15 minutes again after dinner, and three times a day, right on schedule, all week. Then, the next Saturday, he and his dad went to the library to return his books and get new ones. This time he got a book about BMX biking, and he also tried some fiction. Of course, he found another storm book. Week after week, he kept up his schedule of reading, each week with new books. At times his imagination would carry him off to wild and adventurous places. Once he read about hurricane jumpers and imagined he was in the plane with them flying straight into the eye of a hurricane. During that reading session, the ring of the timer almost made him jump off the sofa.

Soon, Russell could tell his reading had improved. He was sure his teacher would be pleased. And Russell was pleased, too. He knew the coming school year would be a lot better.

## Talk About It

What did Russell do to discipline himself to keep reading over the summer? Be specific. Have you ever set and met a goal? If so, how did you feel when you met it?

# The Lead Role

Carmina was thrilled she got the lead in the community play. She was so excited it was all she talked about for two days. On the third day, at recess with her best friend Alicia, she was still talking about it. She talked about her costume, the lines she had to learn, the people she was meeting.

And she talked about how much time it would take to rehearse. "After all, it's a very big part I have," she said importantly. "I may not have as much time to play with you, Alicia."

"Like I'd care," Alicia said under her breath.

Carmina was shocked. "What did you say?" she asked.

"If all you're going to do is brag about how great you are the whole time, you won't be very fun to play with anyway," said Alicia.

"I wasn't bragging!" Carmina protested. But then she thought about the past three days, and she realized Alicia was right. She'd been going on and on about herself. "Well," she said, "maybe just a little."

Alicia smiled at her. "I'm happy for you, Carmina," she said. "It's really awesome that you got the part. But maybe we could talk about something else for a while?"

"Sure," said Carmina. "So what's been going on with you lately?"

## Talk About It

Do you think it was fair of Alicia to be impatient with Carmina? Why or why not? How would you act if you were in a situation like Alicia's? Like Carmina's?

# A Game Plan

As soon as Dan got home from school he turned on his video game and began to play, just like he did every day. Soon he was glued to the screen. He hoped no one would talk to him or disturb him, because he was close to reaching the highest level.

Dan's mom walked into the room to talk. "Dan, I think you need to get outside. All you do is play video games—it's not good for you."

Dan put the game on pause and looked at his mom. "Okay," he said. But he only said it so she would leave and he could get back to his game. As he played he kept thinking about what she said, though. Maybe she *was* right. He used to love playing outside. And he sort of missed his friends. That night, Dan came up with a plan to play video games only two school days a week—not every day like he had been.

The next day after school Dan played catch with his younger brother for a while. Then he tossed a disc with the dog. The next day after school he played video games, and the next day after that he went to the rec center to play basketball with his friends.

At first the change was really hard. But Dan kept to his plan the next week, and the week after that, too. Soon he found that he enjoyed the new variety in his life.

"I'm really proud of you," his mom said one day. "You've shown a lot of discipline."

"I'm proud of me, too, Mom," Dan said.

## Talk About It

What did Dan do that showed he had self-discipline? Why did he do it? Do you think it's important to have more than one activity to do in your free time? Why or why not?

# Trustworthiness

When you are trustworthy you can be depended on. It is important to you not to let others down, and others know that you won't. They know you will be fair, you will keep your word, and you will fulfill your responsibilities.

# The Pet Sitter

Sonny threw the stick as far as he could. Heidi ran fast to fetch it and bring it back. The golden retriever loved to bring Sonny anything he threw. Heidi belonged to the Martins, Sonny's neighbors. He was taking care of their pets while they were gone.

After Sonny brought Heidi back inside, he fed the cats. Then he took the to-do list off the refrigerator and put check marks next to the things he'd done:

1. Walk and feed Heidi.
2. Feed Bootsie and Milo and clean their litter box.
3. Put the mail on the kitchen table.
4. Place newspapers in the box inside the garage.

After he left, he checked the knob to the Martins' front door to make sure he had locked it. Then he walked straight home and hung the key in the kitchen.

The Martins came home that night. Sonny had been pet sitting for them for a whole week. When Ms. Martin came over the next morning, she thanked him for doing such a good job. She said the animals were happy and everything looked in order. "It helped us have a good trip knowing you were taking care of things," she said.

Sonny grinned. He was glad they were happy with the job he had done. "I hope you leave town again soon," he called out to Ms. Martin as she left. They both laughed.

## Talk About It

What do you think Sonny liked about taking care of the Martins' pets? How does it feel when people know they can depend on you? Who are some people *you* depend on? How do you know you can count on them?

# Saturday Softball

April, Sherrie, Helena, and Suz huddled up in front of the school, making plans for a softball game on Saturday. Each girl would invite a couple friends so they would have enough players. They would meet at noon.

"We'll bring cold drinks for everyone," April said. She and Suz lived next door to each other so it would be easy for them to manage the cooler.

"I'll bring the bat and ball," said Sherrie.

"Make sure you do," April chimed in, "or we won't have a game. You're the only one who has a bat."

On Saturday, April and Suz arrived early with the cooler. Other girls began to flock to the field. They marked off the bases and were ready to begin. But they had a major problem—no bat or ball.

"Where's Sherrie?" Helena asked.

Nobody had heard from her.

"No Sherrie, no game," Suz huffed. "Rats!"

Just then Sherrie's big brother, Dak, drove up with Sherrie in the back seat. Slowly she got out of the car. Her big toe was taped up. She had broken it the night before.

"You girls owe me big time," Dak joked. "Sherrie begged me to bring the bat and ball to you—even though I have plenty of *important* things I could be doing right now."

"Does it hurt?" Suz asked.

"Not too bad," said Sherrie. "Mostly I'm just disappointed I won't get to play softball."

"Well, thanks for bringing the stuff," said Helena, taking the bat and ball from Dak. "It would've been easy to just forget the whole thing." The other girls chimed in their thanks, too. Then Dak and Sherrie sat in the bleachers to watch the game.

## Talk About It

Why did Sherrie bring the bat and ball even though she couldn't play? If Sherrie's brother hadn't agreed to drive her, what else could Sherrie have done?

# The Candy Money

Gus paced nervously outside his karate instructor's office. He fiddled with the yellow belt of his white uniform. When the instructor got off the phone, Gus knocked on the door and asked if he could talk to him in private.

Gus's palms were sweating as he walked into the office. Karate trophies lined the shelves. He swallowed hard and handed Mr. Dean a wadded up, damp envelope full of quarters. "Last week I was assigned to count the candy money, and I took this out before I gave you the total," he said in a very low voice. "I wanted to buy a new gel pen and didn't have the money."

"So you took it from the class fund?" his instructor asked, holding up the envelope.

"Yes—I'm sorry," said Gus, twisting his belt. "I felt bad about it all week, so I was really anxious to see you today and return it."

"I appreciate your bringing the money back, Gus. It's never okay to steal, but bringing it back shows that you can be trustworthy."

## Talk About It

Even though Gus confessed, do you think there should be consequences for his stealing? Why or why not? Do you think it's strange that the instructor said Gus showed he can be trustworthy—even though he had stolen money? Why or why not?

# Mum's the Word!

As the bell rang to begin recess, Cody gently grabbed Tabatha by the shoulder. "I have to talk to you at recess," he said.

After they put on their jackets, the two friends walked on the blacktop together. Nearby, other kids were swinging on swings and running on the basketball court. "What is it?" Tabatha asked.

"Well," Cody said nervously. "I wanted to tell you that, um, well—I just wanted to say that I really like Omni."

Tabatha just nodded her head and listened. "Why did you tell me?" she asked.

"I just *had* to tell someone, and I know I can trust you because you always keep your word."

"Of course you can trust me," said Tabatha. "Mum's the word!"

"So you won't tell anyone?"

"Not if you don't want me to," Tabatha said.

"Thanks," Cody said. "It's a *big* secret. But I'm glad I could tell you."

## Talk About It

Why did Cody choose to tell Tabatha how he felt about Omni? Have you ever trusted someone the way Cody trusted Tabatha? Or has someone trusted you that way? How did it work out?

# The Library Trip

"**M**om," Marsha said. "Is it okay if I head over to the library to do my homework?"

"I thought you finished up your research project last week," her mom said.

"I did. I just like it there," Marsha said, zipping up her backpack. "It's quiet and I like being around all those books."

"Are your friends all meeting there or something?" her mom asked.

"No," said Marsha. "We can't talk at the library anyway. It's not fun to hang out with friends there. I just like to sit on the couch and study at the library."

Her mom shut the book she was reading. "I just want to make sure your homework is getting done, Marsha—that's all. If you do it here, I know you're doing it."

"You know I'll do it there, too," Marsha said. "Have I ever let you down?"

Her mom thought about it for a second. "No, you haven't," she said, opening her book again. "Your afternoon plans sound great. Hope you get a lot done."

## Talk About It

Why do you think parents sometimes have trouble trusting kids? What can you do to show others that you can be trusted?

# About the Authors

Photo by Cary Albright

**Anne D. Mather** has a degree in education, has taught school (middle school, high school, and church school), and has authored several books, including *Bridging the Gap*, a guide for teenagers. She serves as a writer and an editor for a journal published by the Centers for Disease Control and Prevention. Anne also was trained as a radio writer by the Associated Press and has an M.A. in journalism.

Photo by Cary Albright

**Louise B. Weldon** has worked on behalf of kids most of her career in varying capacities, including as a workshop presenter (to counselors, social workers, and teachers), teacher trainer, and volunteer. Louise founded and directed the youth program for a large congregation in Atlanta and served as coordinator of the child abuse prevention program for the Woodstock, Georgia, police department, going into elementary schools and presenting programs on child safety. She also served on the Board of Directors for the Cherokee County (Georgia) Advocacy Center for Children. She has taught parenting and self-esteem classes in churches, schools, and universities.

Anne and Louise are previously published coauthors of *The Cat at the Door and Other Stories to Live By*, *The Cats in the Classroom*, *Around the Year with the Cat at the Door* (a teacher workbook), and *Cat Tales* (a journal).

# Other Great Books from Free Spirit

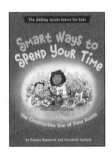